green clean

including vinegar, citrus fruits and b... soda

D0529442

Contents

All rights reserved,

No part of this publication may be reproduced, stored in a retrieval system or transmitted by any means (electronic, mechanical, photocopying or otherwise) without the prior permission of the publisher.

This edition published in 2007 by L&K Designs.
© L&K Designs 2007
PRINTED IN CHINA

Publishers Disclaimer

The uses, hints, tips and ideas contained in this book are passed on in good faith but the publisher cannot be held responsible for any adverse results.

Why "green" clean?

Many chemicals in the cleaning products used each day can harm you and your children. Indoor air carries a higher risk for personal exposure to toxic chemicals than outdoor air. Many of the chemicals in household cleaners and pesticides are not adequately tested, regulated or controlled. An estimated 2 to 5 million exposures to household poisons occur every year, and a significant number of them involve household cleaners.

Many household cleaning products, such as furniture polish, oven cleaners, drain cleaners and even air fresheners are classed as hazardous waste. Almost all commercially available floor and furniture waxes contain neurotoxic petroleum-based solvents. Neurotoxic chemicals can cause headaches, lack of concentration, irritability and more, and are best avoided and substitutes used. Replacing commercial furniture polish with a homemade formula is at the top of the list of priorities for establishing a healthier home, along with replacing oven cleaner and pesticides.

Most households contain dozens of bottles of unnecessary cleaning products. People invest in separate products for individual cleaning jobs: furniture polish, bathroom floor cleaner, bathroom fixture cleaner, kitchen floor cleaner, kitchen fixtures cleaners, oven cleaner, bleach for white clothes, 2-3 laundry detergents for stain removal and dark coloured laundry, glass cleaner and many more. All of these products are costly, dangerous to your home, family and the environment. A household needs only 2-3 homemade organic products with which to keep the entire house sparkling clean! Why organic products? Because they are non-toxic to your pets, family members and the environment. Green cleaning products that you make yourself cost only pennies.

Toxic chemicals in the home can be eliminated simply by making thoughtful choices in the supermarket after educating oneself about where the hazards are in common consumer products. How can you determine what toxics you have in your home? Take this "toxics tour".

In the kitchen

All-purpose cleaner, ammonia-based cleaners, bleach, brass or other metal polishes, dishwasher detergent, disinfectant, drain cleaner, floor wax or polish, glass cleaner, dishwashing detergent, oven cleaner, and scouring powder contain dangerous chemicals. Some examples are:

sodium hypochlorite (in chlorine bleach):

if mixed with ammonia, releases toxic chloramine gas. Short-term exposure may cause mild asthmatic symptoms or more serious respiratory problems;

petroleum distillates (in metal polishes):

short-term exposure can cause temporary eye clouding; longer exposure can damage the nervous system, skin, kidneys, and eyes;

ammonia (in glass cleaner):
eye irritant, can cause headaches and lung irritation;

phenol and cresol (in disinfectants):

corrosive; can cause diarrhoea, fainting, dizziness, and kidney and liver damage;

nitrobenzene (in furniture and floor polishes):

can cause skin discoloration, shallow breathing, vomiting, and death; associated with cancer and birth defects;

formaldehyde (a preservative in many products):

suspected human carcinogen; strong irritant to eyes, throat, skin, and lungs.

In the utility room

A number of products are likely to contain toxic ingredients: carpet cleaner, room deodorizer, laundry softener, laundry detergent, anti-cling sheets, mould and mildew cleaner, mothballs, and spot remover all usually contain irritant or toxic substances. Examples:

perchloroethylene or **1-1-1 trichloroethane solvents**
(in spot removers and carpet cleaners):

can cause liver and kidney damage if ingested; perchloroethylene is an animal carcinogen and suspected human carcinogen;

naphthalene or paradichlorobenzene (in mothballs):

naphthalene is a suspected human carcinogen that may damage eyes, blood, liver, kidneys, skin, and the central nervous system; paradichlorobenzene can harm the central nervous system, liver, and kidneys;

hydrochloric acid or **sodium acid sulfate** (in toilet bowl cleaner):

either can burn the skin or cause vomiting, diarrhoea and stomach burns if swallowed; also can cause blindness if inadvertently splashed in the eyes;

residues from fabric softeners, as well as the fragrances commonly used in them, can be irritating to susceptible people;

possible ingredients of spray starch (aside from the starch) include formaldehyde, phenol, and pentachlorophenol; in addition, any aerosolized particle, including cornstarch, may irritate the lungs.

In the living room and bedroom

Even the furnishings of the typical Western home can be harmful. Fabrics that are labelled "wrinkle-resistant" are usually treated with a formaldehyde resin.

These include no-iron sheets and bedding, curtains, sleep wear – any woven fabric, but especially polyester/cotton blends, marketed as "permanent press" or "easy care".

More modern furniture is made of pressed wood products which emits formaldehyde and other chemicals. Carpeting is usually made of synthetic fibres that have been treated with pesticides and fungicide. Many office carpets emit a chemical called 4-phenylcyclohexene, an inadvertent additive to the latex backing used in more commercial carpets, which is thought to be one of the chemicals responsible for "sick" office buildings.

We all know the smell – lemon with a touch of engine oil – that we identify as furniture polish. What we may not identify with the smell is the irritability, depression, and other bad moods that can be the response to its use. How many people polish their furniture before a dinner party, only to wonder why they are so cranky before the guests arrive? Even worse, the smell of furniture polish can linger on furniture for weeks and months after use, causing a low level of air pollution that puts a strain on the central nervous systems of everyone living there. The petroleum distillates and solvents in commercial furniture polish are highly neurotoxic.

In the bathroom

Numerous cosmetics and personal hygiene products contain hazardous substances. Examples:

cresol, formaldehyde, glycols, nitrates/nitrosamines and sulfur compounds in shampoos;

butane propellants in hair spray (replacing carcinogenic methylene chloride), as well as formaldehyde resins;

aerosol propellants, ammonia, formaldehyde, triclosan, aluminium chlorhydrate in antiperspirants and deodorants;

glycols, phenol, fragrance, and colours in lotions, creams, and moisturizers.

In the studio

Although legislation controlling many of the dangerous ingredients in hobby materials has recently been passed, exposure to certain art materials remains a health risk. Dangerous chemicals and metals include:

lead in ceramic glazes, stained-glass materials, and many pigments;

cadmium in silver solders, pigments, ceramic glazes and fluxes;

chromium in paint pigments and ceramic colours;

manganese dioxide in ceramic colours and some brown oil and acrylic paint pigments;

cobalt in some blue oil and acrylic paint pigments;

formaldehyde as a preservation in many acrylic paints and photographic products;

hydrocarbons in paint and varnish removers, aerosol sprays, permanent markers, etc.;

chlorinated hydrocarbons (solvents) in ink, varnish, and paint removers, rubber cement, aerosol sprays;

petroleum distillates (solvents) in paint and rubber cement thinners, spray adhesives, silk-screen inks;

glycol ethers and acetates in photography products, lacquer thinners, paints, and aerosol sprays.

In the garage

A number of dangerous substances are frequently present, including paint, paint thinner, benzene, kerosene, mineral spirits, turpentine, lubricating/motor oils, and gasoline. Hazards among them include these chemicals:

chlorinated aliphatic and aromatic hydrocarbons in paint thinner can cause liver and kidney damage;

petroleum hydrocarbons, an ingredient of gasoline, motor oils, and benzene, are associated with skin and lung cancer;

mineral spirits in oil-based paint are a skin, eye, nose throat, and lung irritant. High air concentrations can cause nervous system damage, unconsciousness and death;

ketones in paint thinner may cause respiratory ailments; vary according to specific form of the chemical;

ketones and toluene in wood putty; toluene is highly toxic, may cause skin, kidney, liver, central nervous system damage; may damage reproductive system.

In the garden

Pesticides are one of the most important single hazards in the home.

Around 1400 pesticides, herbicides, and fungicides are ingredients in consumer products. Combined with other toxic substances such as solvents, pesticides are present in more than 34,000 different product formulations.

If you use a barbeque you should be aware that charcoal lighter fluid contains petroleum distillates. Besides being flammable and imparting a chemical taste to food, some petroleum distillates contain benzene, a known human carcinogen.

Ingredients & Recipes

Basic Ingredients

There are many inexpensive, easy-to-use natural cleaning alternatives which can be used safely in place of commercial household cleaning products. One shelf of simple and relatively safe ingredients can be used to perform most home cleaning chores. All that's needed is a knowledge of how they work and how different ingredients should be combined to get the cleaning power needed for a specific job.

Here are ordinary, environmentally safe ingredients which can be used alone or in combination for a wealth of household cleaning applications.

Baking soda

Baking soda is sodium bicarbonate. It is a common ingredient used in baking that can be used as an all-purpose, non-toxic cleaner. It is effective at removing stains and it is also a mild scouring tool for pots, pans and sink basins. It can neutralize acid, soften hard water and fabrics and extinguish grease fires. It can be used as a deodorizer around the home including in the refrigerator, on smelly carpets, on upholstery, on vinyl and down drains. It can clean and polish aluminium, chrome, jewellery, plastic, porcelain, silver, stainless steel, and tin.

Beeswax

Beeswax is secreted by worker bees whilst building the honeycomb, and is a pleasantly scented natural product. Traditionally beeswax has been used in wood polishes. It gives furniture a great shine, a protective coat, and helps the wood develop a patina. In addition, the wax can be used as a lubricant for drawers and windows. Beeswax is highly flammable, so it is important to follow certain procedures and precautions whenever melting it down for use in a polish recipe. Overheating beeswax can damage it and be hazardous. To avoid overheating, always place the container or small saucepan of wax, inside a larger pan of water. Never place a pan of wax directly on a hot plate or gas ring, and never heat beeswax over a direct flame. Beeswax melts at 63° C to 65° C. It does not boil, and if it is overheated it could ignite, and burn ferociously. In the event of fire, do not use water to extinguish the flames. Use sand, a large damp cloth or a fire extinguisher. Beeswax should only be melted in stainless steel or tin plated containers. (Other metals can taint the colour.)

Borax

Borax is a naturally occurring mineral, soluble in water. An alternative to bleach, it can deodorize, inhibit the growth of mildew and mould, boost the cleaning power of soap or detergent, remove stains, and can be used with attractants such as sugar to kill cockroaches. Borax cleans, softens water, and disinfects and in the laundry room will go a long way toward adding freshness to your clothes.

Castile and vegetable oil based soaps

Find a soap in liquid, solid or powder form that is biodegradable, free of dyes and non-petroleum based. Castile or other plant-based soaps are a great choice and can be used to clean everything. Olive-oil based soap is gentlest to the skin.

An all-purpose liquid soap can be made by simple dissolving the old ends of bar soap, or grated slivers of bar soap, in warm water. (If doing this remember to avoid using soaps which contain petroleum distillates.)

Citrus solvent

Citrus solvent cleans paint brushes, oil and grease, and some stains.

Cornstarch

Cornstarch derived from corn, can be used to clean windows, polish furniture, shampoo carpets and rugs, absorb oil and grease and starch clothes.

Cream of tartar

Cream of tartar is a mild acid often used in baking, and it can be used for removing tough stains in your kitchen or bath.

Essential oils

Caution: Pregnant women, diabetics, and people with other medical conditions should consult with a doctor about using essential oils.

Essential oils can be used for disinfecting and fragrance. As far back as ancient Egyptian and Greek times, people used lavender, rosemary, tansy, and other herbs for cleaning. They freshened their linens by placing fragrant sachets, herbs, and flowers in drawers and closets.

Homes were "sweetened" with garlands of lavender and mint. Essential oils are great for adding fragrance and disinfecting properties to your homemade cleaning sprays. Lavender, orange, rosemary and clove are wonderful scents for your home. You can combine oils to create citrus, floral or spicy fragrances.

Essential oils should be handled with care. They are strong volatile oils and can be hazardous to you and your family. Store them away from pets and children. Pregnant women, diabetics, and people with other medical conditions should always consult with a doctor about using essential oils.

Eucalyptus essential oil
This is great for cutting grease, for example it works great on those rings around the bathtub, grease on mirrors, grease on counters and such like. It will also cut soap scum. It is antibacterial, antifungal, antiviral and beneficial to the immune system. Also good on grease are tea tree oil, lavender, lemon and orange.

Lavender essential oil
People seem to have a natural inclination toward lavender's sweet, woody aroma. Lavender has age-old housekeeping uses and gifts. It has great cleaning properties and is antibacterial, antifungal, antiviral, and boosts the immune system. Nearly everyone can use it with no allergic reaction. If you are very sensitive to everything and are tired of having no fragrance around try a little pure organic lavender essential oil in your cleaning products.

Lemon essential oil
Lemon oil has antiviral, antibacterial, antifungal and cleansing properties. It works well on odours and it is also claimed to have whitening properties, although lemon juice is probably better in this respect. Most commercial lemon oil is not all natural, but may contain petroleum distillates. Contact herbalists for pure sources of lemon oil. Traditionally, lemon oil has been used for furniture because it is so lubricating and antiseptic.

Jasmine essential oil
This works great as a cleaner and a whitener. It will also kill mould and mildew.

Thyme essential oil
This is antifungal, antiviral, antibacterial and boosts the immune system. It is becoming very popular as the new disinfectant.

Herbs
Many herbs have beneficial cleaning properties and not only will your house be clean and fragrant, you will also get the benefit of herbal aromatherapy during the cleaning process! Making a herbal infusion is like making a strong tea. Boil some water and add 1 tablespoon to one cup of water for about 10 minutes. Let it stand for an hour then pour into a glass jar and use that in your cleaning products. This must be kept refrigerated and will go bad after about two weeks.

Choose the herb with the characteristics needed for each task from the following list. Then use them in the recipes given below:

Antiseptic
all bactericide herbs plus basil, clary sage, clove, lemon balm, peppermint, rose geranium, sage, spearmint

Bactericide
bay, cinnamon, eucalyptus, lavender, oregano, patchouli, rosemary, savory, tea tree, thyme

Disinfectant Herbs
basil, chamomile, clary sage, eucalyptus, lavender, peppermint, rose geranium, thyme

Fungicide
chamomile, lemon, peppermint, rosemary, savory, tea tree, thyme

Insect Repellents
basil, bay, chamomile, coriander, tansy, thyme, rosemary, peppermint, lavender

Hydrogen peroxide
Hydrogen peroxide is more gentle than chlorine bleach and can be used for sterilizing and disinfecting, both in your home and on your body.

Lemon juice
Lemon juice, which contains citric acid, is a deodorant and can be used to clean glass and remove stains from aluminium and porcelain. It cuts through grease and removes perspiration and other stains from clothing and it is a mild lightener or bleach if used with sunlight.

Lemon juice can be used to dissolve soap scum and hard water deposits. Lemon is a great substance to clean and shine brass and copper. Lemon juice can be mixed with vinegar and or baking soda to make cleaning pastes.

Cut a lemon in half and sprinkle baking soda on the cut section. Use the lemon to scrub dishes, surfaces, and stains.

Lime juice
Is also a powerful natural acidic cleaner which is good for removing mineral build-up and grease. Limes can be used in much the same way as lemons in nontoxic cleaning.

Mineral oil
Mineral oil, derived from seeds, is an ingredient in several furniture polish and floor wax recipes.

Olive oil
Olive oil is great for moisturizing and conditioning leather furniture and as a furniture polish.

Orange oil
Orange oil consists of about 90% d-Limonene, a solvent used in various household chemicals, such as to condition wooden furniture, and along with other citrus oils in grease removal and as a hand-cleansing agent. It is an efficient cleaning agent which is much less toxic than petroleum distillates. It also smells great!

Salt (sodium chloride)

Salt is one of the most versatile ingredients for green cleaning given its abrasive and bleaching properties. It is also a natural deodorizer and when mixed with vinegar and flour creates an excellent cleaning paste.

Steel wool

Steel wool is an abrasive strong enough to remove rust and stubborn food residues and to scour barbeque grills.

Tea tree oil

The essential oil known as "tea tree oil" comes from the melaleuca tree, a shrub/tree that has needle-like leaves. There are 100 varieties of melaleuca, but for the purposes of this book we are speaking of Australian tea tree oil, or melaleuca alternifolia. Tea tree works well to kill mould and mildew as it is a natural fungicide and germicide, and is naturally antibacterial and antiseptic. It is great for home care as well as personal care. Tea tree oil may help to treat fungus disorders like athlete's foot and toe nail infections as well as yeast infections and acne.

Toothpaste

Toothpaste is a mild abrasive, and particularly good for cleaning silverware and ornaments, though is not recommended for use on fine jewellery.

TSP (trisodium phosphate)

TSP is a mixture of soda ash and phosphoric acid. TSP is toxic if swallowed, but it can be used on many jobs, such as cleaning drains or removing old paint, that would normally require much more caustic and poisonous chemicals, and it does not create any fumes.

Washing soda (sodium carbonate)

Washing soda or SAL Soda is a sodium carbonate decahydrate, a mineral. It can be used with soda instead of laundry detergent, and it softens hard water. It can cut stubborn grease, such as on grills, pans, and ovens. It can also be used to clean walls, tiles, sinks and baths or sinks. When using washing soda, it can irritate mucous membranes and can also irritate the skin so use rubber gloves when putting hands directly into a washing soda solution. Do not use on aluminium.

Vinegar

Vinegar is made from soured fruit juice, grain, or wine. It contains about 5 per cent acetic acid, which makes it a mild acid. The disinfectant properties of vinegar have been verified by numerous studies. Besides its disinfectant properties, there are many uses for vinegar around the household. Vinegar cuts grease, removes stains and is an excellent water softener. Vinegar can dissolve mineral deposits, grease, remove traces of soap, remove mildew or wax buildup, polish some metals, and deodorize. Vinegar can clean brick or stone, and is an ingredient in some natural carpet cleaning recipes. Vinegar is normally used in a solution with water, but it can be used straight.

White vinegar

White vinegar is a great disinfecting tool. It can be used for disinfecting, deodorizing, cutting grease and wax build-up, removing mildew, and removing stains on carpets, countertops, pots, pans and coffee carafes.

Recycle

In addition to using only green ingredients in your cleaners, to ensure that you are helping the environment to remain toxic free there are a few simple things that you can do:

Cloth

Use cloth rags; never use paper towels or the new "disposable wipes". Such products are bleached, and are therefore toxins. Recycle old clothing, sheets and towels into rags. Wash once a week and you'll never have to waste money on paper products again.

Plastic

Recycle paper and plastic bags and never buy plastic bin bags. Use the bags that you get from the supermarket to dispose of cat litter and household waste. Invest in cloth bags to use for groceries, and take only 1-2 plastic or paper bags from the supermarket to use as bin bags. Paper bags are the most environmentally friendly, however some areas have ordinances against using paper bags for rubbish pick-ups. Minimize your use of plastic.

Be resourceful with your time. Clean starting from top to bottom i.e. ceiling to furniture to floors, except in the kitchen and bathrooms where you should sweep the floors first. (When water gets onto a dirty floor then it is harder to clean up.) Clean from one side of the room and move around in a circle. When cleaning don't forget the often overlooked or forgotten areas such as ceiling fans, high surfaces, light fixtures, lamps, blinds, windowsills, the laundry room, the inside of bins, the inside of the microwave, and salt and pepper shakers.

RECIPES

Caution: Pregnant women, diabetics, and people with other medical conditions should consult with a doctor about using essential oils.

Do homemade cleaners work? Yes. Non-toxic cleaners are naturally milder, so you cannot just spray them on and watch the dirt dissolve away, as you can with some of the powerful toxic chemicals, but many of the recipes work just as well if not better than the chemical alternatives.

To save time and money, make your cleaners in advance and buy the ingredients in bulk for cost savings and to avoid excess packaging. Make large batches of the recipes and store them in reusable airtight plastic containers and spray bottles.

You can add your favourite essential oils or herbs to many of these formulas for fragrance.

Although the ingredients you will be using to make your own cleaning products are of organic origin, that doesn't mean they are without consequences if ingested. Please exercise the same caution with your homemade cleaning products as you would with any commercial cleaner. Ensure your products are clearly labelled and keep them away from pets and children.

In general, it is also recommended that although these are green products, gloves should be worn to reduce the possibility of skin irritations. Also, when cleaning ensure that windows are kept open to reduce the build up of fumes. Plan to keep the following around:

- Plastic squirt bottles of various sizes
- Plastic spray bottles
- Misters (plastic pump spray bottles)
- Coffee cans with lids
- Glass jars with screw-top lids
- Cotton cloths (to use instead of paper towels)
- Rags
- Cellulose sponge cloths

Basic Rules for Making Natural Cleaners

1.   Label your cleaners properly and include the ingredients.

2.   Don't reuse the containers of commercial cleaning products as there may still be residues of the nasty chemicals.

3.   Never ever mix commercial products with your homemade products – you don't know what you could create.

4.   Don't use ammonia.

5.   Store them away from children and pets.

Please don't eat or drink any of your cleaners!!

Air Fresheners/Deodorizers

Air freshener spray
Mix white distilled vinegar and an essential oil for fragrance, and use in a 275ml/1/2 pint fine mist spray bottle.

Air-purifying spray
For an air-purifying spray, mix essential oils of eucalyptus, lemon and thyme with water in a spray bottle, then spritz your germ-filled rooms.

Gel Fragrance in a jar
Make your own gel air freshener with a few simple ingredients.
225ml/1 cup water (divided)
1 packet gelatin
1/8 teaspoon rubbing alcohol or vodka
1/2 teaspoon essential oil or fragrance oil.

Boil 110ml/1/2 cup water, then dissolve the gelatin in it. Add the other half of the water (cold) and stir until blended. Add the alcohol and essential oil and stir until well blended. Pour into jars of your choice. Don't place on a very warm spot like the top of the TV or it will liquify some. If this happens, you can restore it by placing in the refrigerator for a while.

Air Fresheners/Deodorizers

Lemon and baking soda spray
Dissolve baking soda in 450ml/2 cups hot water, add lemon juice, pour into spray bottle, and spray into air as air freshener

Lavendor room aromatherapy
Lavender contains esters and aldehydes that help to regulate your mood, and it is widely used by herbalists to treat depression. Place a few drops in a water vaporizer, or on a light bulb.

All-purpose Cleaners/General Household Cleaners

For a quick and easy surface cleaner, mix together vinegar and salt. Also baking soda can be used on a damp sponge to clean and deodorize all kitchen and bathroom surfaces.

For a general cleaner dissolve 4 tablespoons baking soda in 1 1/2ltrs/2 1/2 pints of warm water. Recipes for other all-purpose cleaners are as follows:

All-purpose cleaner no. 1
3 tablespoons vinegar
1/2 teaspoon washing soda
1/2 teaspoon vegetable oil based liquid soap
450ml/2 cups hot water

Mix ingredients in spray bottle or bucket. Apply and wipe clean.

All-purpose cleaner no. 2
1 tablespoon borax
55ml/1/4 cup vinegar
900ml/4 cups hot water
You can also add a dash of liquid soap

When cleaning the whole house, mix together these ingredients to make an all-purpose cleaner that can be used on countertops, sinks, tubs, tiles and anywhere else you need to disinfect.

All-purpose spray cleaner

1/2 teaspoon washing soda
1/2 teaspoon borax
1/2 teaspoon vegetable oil-based soap
2 tablespoons vinegar
450ml/2 cups of hot water

Combine in a spray bottle: Shake well until all the solid bits have dissolved. For extra cleaning power increase borax to 1 teaspoon. Spray and wipe clean with a damp cloth or sponge.

Apple cider all-purpose cleaner

Apple cider vinegar can be staining but less people are allergic to it than white vinegar. Lemon juice can be substituted but it must be kept refrigerated. To make an old fashioned apple cider all-purpose cleaner you will need to have a spray bottle on hand.

1 cup apple cider vinegar or lemon juice
(or use more if you want it to be stronger)
Fill the rest up with water
10 to 20 drops of your favourite essential oil (optional) or boil some herbs and pour that in (this will not last longer than 2 weeks)
one tablespoon of liquid Castile soap (optional)
5 to 10 drops of grapefruit seed extract (also optional)

Directions: Spray and wipe. Use as a daily shower spray to cut down on soap scum. Just spray, leave on for 20 minutes and wipe with a towel, or spray and leave to dry. Use as an all-purpose cleaner for your kitchen counters, appliances, floors, windows, mirrors. It can also be used on window sills and to wash a floor, pour about 110ml/1/2 cup in a bucket of water to mop any floor. This versatile cleaner can also be used in your dishwasher as a dish rinse or in the laundry as a rinse.

General Tea Tree Oil Spray

Combine 2 teaspoons of tea tree oil in 1160ml/2 cups of water in a spray bottle. Shake to blend. This has multiple uses around the house. For use on mould, spray on the affected area and don't rinse. The smell will dissipate in a few days. The smell of mould and damp will be gone, too, never to return as long as the source of moisture has been removed. It can also be used as a Household Antiseptic Spray to spray areas that need antiseptic attention, such as after someone has vomited.

Liquid natural detergent

To make 1 gallon of liquid natural detergent for use in the dishwasher, on floors, for laundry and on the bathtub and tiles:

115g/1 cup of Castile soap
40g/1/3 cup of salt
115g/1 cup of dissolved borax or baking soda (optional)
225ml/1 cup of vinegar (optional)
40 drops of grapefruit seed extract (optional)
papaya enzymes – about 4 crushed capsules per gallon

If your skin is very sensitive then just stick to the salt and Castile soap and the grapefruit seed extract, or experiment with it.

Fill your gallon jug up halfway with water. You can pour half of the water into a bowl and reserve it. Dissolve your salt, baking soda or borax in a pan of water. Warm the water on the stove on low heat and stir until it is dissolved. Add to your gallon jug along with the Castile soap and the optional vinegar. Fill your jug up the rest of the way. Add essential oils and grapefruit extract. Shake the jug.

The cleaner can be used for baths, sinks, toilet bowls and both wall and floor tiles by gently rubbing and then rinsing with clean water. To clean floors add 110-225ml/1/2-1 cup to your bucket of water and clean any floor except laminate. It can be used in your dishwasher in place of dishwashing detergent, your washing machine in place of laundry detergent and when used on glass surfaces creates a beautiful shine.

Bathroom Cleaning

In addition to the general all purpose cleaners, here are some specific recipes for cleaning the bathroom.

Bathroom soft scrub
115g/1 cup of baking soda or borax or washing soda
115g/1 cup of Castile soap

Mix together and use as a soft scrub for your sink, bath, tiles and in the toilet. Rinse with clean water.

Toilet bowl cleaner no. 1
115g/1 cup borax
110ml/1/2 cup white vinegar

Flush to wet the sides of the bowl. Sprinkle the borax around the toilet bowl, then spray with vinegar. Leave for several hours or overnight before scrubbing with a toilet brush.

Toilet bowl cleaner no. 2
liquid Castile soap
baking soda or borax

Simply pour down the bowl and scrub with a toilet brush.

Bath, sink and tile cleaner no. 1
190g/1 2/3 cups baking soda
110ml/1/2 cup liquid soap
2 tablespoons vinegar
110ml/1/2 cup water
a few drops of tea tree essential oil

Mix soda and soap. Add water, then add vinegar and oil. Store in a squirt-top bottle and shake before using. Rinse thoroughly to avoid leaving a residue.

Bath, sink and tile cleaner no. 2

Combine 115g/1/2 cup baking soda with enough vegetable oil-based liquid soap to make a frosting like mixture. Add 15 drops of tea tree oil. Scoop the mixture onto a sponge and scrub the bath, sinks, countertops or shower stall. Rinse well with clean water.

Carpet Deodorizers

Carpet freshener

460g/4 cups baking soda or cornstarch
35 drops eucalyptus essential oil
30 drops lavender essential oil
25 drops rosewood essential oil
or any combination of your favourite essential oils

Measure 460g/4 cups of baking soda into a bowl, add essential oils. Break up any clumps that form, stir until well mixed. Before vacuuming sprinkle powder from a shaker type can or jar. Let it sit on the carpet for about 15 minutes then vacuum.

Herbal carpet freshener

115g/1 cup baking soda
60g/1/2 cup lavender flowers

Crush the lavender flowers to release their scent. Mix well with baking soda and sprinkle liberally on carpets. Vacuum after 30 minutes.

Dishwashing

Natural dishwashing liquid no. 1

30g/1/4 cup soap flakes
450ml/2 cups hot water
55ml/1/4 cup glycerin
1/2 teaspoon lemon essential oil

In bowl combine soap flakes and water and stir until the soap is dissolved. Cool to lukewarm. Stir in the glycerin and the essential oil, leave to cool.

Natural dishwashing liquid no. 1 - cont/...

As it cools it will form a loose gel. Stir with a fork and break up the gel and then pour into a narrow-necked bottle. To use, squirt 3 teaspoonfuls into hot running water.

Natural dishwashing liquid no. 2

liquid Castile soap
10 drops lavender essential oil
8 drops rosemary essential oil
4 drops eucalyptus essential oil

Fill a clean 650ml/22oz plastic squirt bottle with Castile soap (diluted according to directions if using concentrate). Add the essential oils. To use, squirt 3 teaspoonfuls into hot running water.

Natural automatic dishwasher detergent

110ml/1/2 cup liquid Castile soap
110ml/1/2 cup water
1 teaspoon fresh lemon juice
3 drops tea tree extract (or oil)
55ml/1/4 cup white vinegar
baking soda

Mix together all ingredients except the baking soda. Store in squeeze bottle. Use 1 tablespoon in the first cycle and 1 tablespoon in the automatic soap dispenser for standard size dishwasher. Sprinkle a handful of baking soda over dirty dishes and in the bottom of your dishwasher to absorb odours and boost cleaning power at the start.

Disinfectants, anti-bacterial sprays and natural bleaches

Disinfectant means anything that will reduce the number of harmful bacteria on a surface. Practically no surface treatment will completely eliminate bacteria. Regular cleaning with plain soap and hot water will kill some bacteria.

Disinfectant no. 1
Borax has long been recognized for its disinfectant and deodorizing properties. Mix 55g/1/2 cup borax into 4lts/1 gallon hot water or undiluted vinegar and clean with this solution.

Disinfectant no. 2
2 tablespoons borax
55ml/1/4 cup lemon juice
450ml/2 cups hot water

Combine the borax and lemon juice with the water in a spray bottle. Use as you would any commercial all-purpose cleaner.

Disinfectant no. 3
Isopropyl alcohol is an excellent disinfectant. Sponge on and allow to dry. Use in a well-ventilated area and wear gloves. Keep it away from children.

Disinfectant spray
450ml/2 cups water
55ml/1/4 cup white vinegar
1/4 teaspoon tea tree oil
1/4 teaspoon lavender oil

Combine and store in a spray bottle. Shake occasionally. Use wherever a disinfectant spray is needed.

Lavender anti-bacterial spray
Lavender contains up to 50 per cent of an ingredient called linalool which kills bacteria and viruses. Put 20 drops of pure essential oil of lavender in 1 cup of water, and spray the air, table tops, door knobs etc., anywhere you would usually use a disinfectant.

Natural bleach alternative
For a good natural bleach alternative take a 4ltr/1 gallon jug, fill jug up halfway with water, add 225ml/1 cup of Castile soap, then dilute 40g/1/3 cup of salt and 60g/1/2 cup of baking soda and add 225ml/1 cup of vinegar. Shake and finish filling up with water.

Floors

General floor cleaner

In a bucket mix 110ml/1/2 cup white vinegar with 4ltrs/1 gallon hot water. This is safe for hardwood, linoleum, tile, and any washable surface.

Natural kitchen floor cleaner

225ml/1 cup vinegar
30g/1/4 cup washing soda
1 tablespoon vegetable oil-based liquid soap
8ltrs/2 gallons hot water

Combine all ingredients, stirring well to dissolve the washing soda. Mop as usual.

Wood floor wax

A wax is a semi-solid which will feed and seal wood. For best results make sure the wood is absolutely dry.

225ml/1 cup base oil
110ml/1/2 cup vodka
25-38g/1 - 1 1/2 oz. grated beeswax
38-50g/1 1/2 - 2oz. carnauba wax (depends on hardness desired)
20 drops of essential lavender oil

NB: Carnauba wax is brittle and can be quickly pulverized by placing in a plastic bag and gently tapping with a hammer or other suitable tool.

Put the base oil and the waxes into the top of the double boiler and place over the bottom portion of the double boiler to which water is already added and is at a simmer. At "low heat" stir gently until all waxes are dissolved. Remove from heat and add vodka and essential oil and blend well. Pour into a clean, recycled nut can or other similar size heat-resistant container. Allow to harden. Use a rag to rub into the wood. If the rag "drags" too much, dip it into a tiny bit of the base oil.

Furniture, leather and vinyl

Basic polishing cream waxing formula

Here is a simple, elegant polish formula to make yourself that is solvent free, inexpensive, and easy enough to make.

75ml/2 1/2oz. olive oil or jojoba
45ml/1 1/2 oz. coconut oil
25g/1oz. beeswax
25g/1oz. carnauba wax
120ml/4oz. distilled water

Melt the oils and waxes in a double boiler over medium heat. Remove from the heat, pour in the water, and mix with a hand mixer until thick and creamy. Dab some cream onto a soft cotton rag and rub into the furniture. Buff and polish until the oils are well worked into the wood. This cleaner will have a shelf life of around 6-12 months.

Lavender furniture wax

50g/2oz. grated beeswax
1 tablespoon carnauba wax
235ml/1 1/2 cup mineral spirits
20 drops oil of lavender

Melt waxes in top of double boiler. Let cool 30 seconds or so, then add mineral spirits and oil. Stir well then place in suitable container.

Lemon oil furniture duster

10 drops pure essential lemon oil
2 tablespoons lemon juice
A few drops olive oil or jojoba

Dip a soft recycled cloth, such as flannel, in the lemon oil mixture, and wipe furniture. Allow to dry naturally.

Furniture polish (also leather and vinyl cleaner and conditioner)
725ml/3 1/3 cups of olive oil
40g/1/3 cup Castile soap
40 to 60 drops of essential oil (optional)
10 drops of grapefruit seed extract

Get your 4.5ltr/1 gallon jug of water and start by filling it halfway up with water. Add all your ingredients. Fill the rest of the way up with water. Shake well. Put in a spritzer bottle for best results. This needs to be shaken before each use. These proportions will create about 4.5lts/1 gallon of polish which will keep for up to a year and can, in addition to the uses above, be used for shining stainless steel and on painted surfaces and blinds.

Caution: Not recommended for antiques, or floors.

Wooden furniture polish no. 1
This polish should to be made fresh each time you use it.
1 lemon
1 teaspoon olive oil
1 teaspoon water

Extract the juice from the lemon. Mix with oil and water. Apply a thin coat on your wood surface and let sit for five minutes. Use a soft cloth to buff to a deep shine.

Wooden furniture polish no. 2
Use 3 parts light mineral oil and 1 part olive oil and a drop of lemon juice.

Wooden furniture polish no. 3
30ml/1/8 cup food grade linseed oil
30ml/1/8 cup vinegar
60ml/1/4 cup lemon juice

Mix ingredients, using soft cloth, rub into wood.

Wooden furniture polish no. 4

This works equally well on wood effect/laminated products as well as real wood. The vinegar smell disappears quickly leaving the clean smell of lavender behind. This is a tiny recipe, but a little of it goes a long way and there's no point in mixing and storing a large batch unless you use it quite frequently.

30ml/1/8 cup lavender base oil (or plain olive or other vegetable oil)
1 tablespoon cider vinegar
1 tablespoon vodka
10 drops oil of lavender

Mix all together well in a 120ml/4oz. squirt top bottle, apply and rub into the wood with a clean soft rag.

Vinyl cleaner

1 teaspoon to 30g/1/4 cup washing soda, and 225ml/1 cup boiling water. Dissolve the washing soda in the boiling water. Apply with sponge, wipe off with a damp cloth.

Kitchen

All Purpose Grease cutter

1/2 teaspoon washing soda
1/2 teaspoon vegetable oil-based liquid soap
3 tablespoons vinegar
450ml/2 cups hot water

Mix in spray bottle, spray and scrub, wipe clean.

Appliance cleaner no. 1

450ml/2 cups water
30g/1/4 cup oil-based soap
10 drops rosemary, lavender, or citrus essential oil

Combine all ingredients in a plastic spray bottle. Shake well before each use. Spray generously on appliance surface and wipe with a damp cloth or sponge. Wipe dry with a cloth or towel.

Appliance cleaner no. 2

1 teaspoon borax
3 tablespoons vinegar
450ml/2 cups hot water

Combine in a spray bottle. Shake to mix and dissolve borax. Spray on appliances and wipe off with a soft cloth or sponge.

Microwave cleaner no. 1

30g/1/4 cup baking soda
1 teaspoon vinegar
5-6 drops thyme, lemongrass, or lemon essential oil

Combine all ingredients to make a paste. Apply to the walls and floor of the microwave with a soft cloth or sponge. Rinse well and leave the microwave door open to air-dry for about 25-minutes.

Microwave cleaner no. 2

225ml/1 cup water
1.2ltrs/2 pints quart warm water
30g/1/4 cup baking soda

To loosen dried-on food, put 225ml/1 cup water in a microwavable cup and heat in the microwave until it boils; turn off the microwave and let the water sit for 1 minute. Dissolve baking soda in 1.2ltrs/2 pints warm water and, using a sponge or cloth, wash the interior of the microwave with this solution to clean and deodorize it.

Oven Cleaner

1.2ltrs/2 pints warm water
2 teaspoons borax
2 tablespoons liquid soap

Spray on solution, wait 20 minutes, then clean with rag and rinse with clean water.

Scourers and scrubbers

Some ready to hand green scouring powders are baking soda or dry table salt. These are mild abrasives and can be used as an alternative to chlorine scouring powders. Simply put either baking soda or salt on a sponge or the surface, scour and rinse. For another inexpensive scouring powder, combine two tablespoons each of vinegar and baking soda. Here is a recipe for a non abrasive scrubber

Soft scrubber, non-abrasive

30g/1/4 cup borax
vegetable-oil based liquid soap
1/2 teaspoon lemon oil

In a bowl, mix the borax with enough soap to form a creamy paste. Add lemon oil and blend well. Scoop a small amount of the mixture onto a sponge, wash the surface, then rinse well.

Laundry

Dryer sheets no. 1

1/2 part lavender essential oil
1/2 part benzoin essential oil (absolute resin)
small dropper bottle
1 scrap of cotton cloth (about 4 inches square)

Make base essential oil by mixing the two oils in equal amounts into a small dropper bottle. Shake well. Label. Put 4-5 drops onto the cloth and place in the dryer.

Dryer sheets no. 2

Take 10-15 4-inch square cloths and put 4-5 drops of essential oil base on each one. Put into an airtight container that you can easily get your hand into to take one out at a time as needed for the dryer.

Use as you would a normal dryer sheet. The airtight container will help hold the scent in the dryer sheets instead of just dissipating out into the room and leaving the dryer sheet less scented.

Dryer sheets no. 3
15 drops of spearmint
12 drops of lavender

Put this mixture on a clean cloth and then fold the cloth several times. Wrap another cloth around that and use in the dryer.

Fabric softener no. 1
230g/2 cups baking soda
450ml/2 cups white vinegar
900ml/4 cups water

Mix these ingredients and use 55ml/1/4 cup per load in the final rinse.

Fabric softener no. 2
4.5ltrs/1 gallon vinegar
20 drops lavender essential oil

Add the lavender essential oil to the vinegar right in the container and you've got instant fabric softener. Shake well before using. For a large load, add 225ml/1 cup during the rinse cycle; use 110ml/1/2 cup during the rinse cycle for smaller loads.

Laundry detergent
15ml/1oz. liquid Castile soap
115g/1 cup washing soda
115g/1 cup baking soda
225ml/1 cup white vinegar

Fill washer with water and add each ingredient in the order given. Launder as usual.

Lavender Water for Linens
675ml/3 cups of distilled water
85ml/3 oz ethyl alcohol (or isopropyl or 100% proof vodka)
15-30 drops essential oil of lavender

Pour the water and alcohol into the container and then add the lavender oil and stir. This water will ferment over time and should last about a year. This lavender linen water can be used when pressing your linens, especially pillowcases, to infuse with its soothing, rest-inducing scent. Just add the scented water to your iron, as you would water to use the steam function.

Mirrors and windows

Glass cleaner, non-streak
55ml/1/4 cup white vinegar
1 tablespoon cornstarch
1.2ltrs/2 pints warm water

Mix the ingredients and apply with a sponge or pour into spray bottle and spray on. Wipe dry with crumpled newspaper, buff to a shine.

Mirror cleaner
335ml/1 1/2 cups vinegar
110ml/1/2 cup water
8 drops citrus essential oil of choice

Combine all ingredients in a spray bottle and shake well before use. Spray solution onto mirror and wipe with a dry cloth or towel.

Window cleaner
Place the following in a spritzer bottle and shake well. Use as you would any window cleaner product.

1/3 teaspoon liquid Castile or other liquid vegetable based soap
3 tablespoons cider vinegar or white vinegar
450ml/2 cups water

Create your own recipes and write them here:-

Name: -

Ingredients: -

- -

- -

Useage: -

- -

- -

Name: -

Ingredients: -

- -

- -

Useage: -

- -

- -

Name: -

Ingredients: -

- -

- -

Useage: -

- -

- -

Kitchen

Kitchen

Rather than use a different cleaning product for the hob, kitchen sink, cabinets, floor and refrigerator, there are only 4 products that you need, and you can purchase the products in any grocery store. They are white vinegar, baking soda, lemon juice and salt.

Cleaning the kitchen

Baking dishes – enamel, ceramic or glass
Soak in hot soapy water, then scour with salt or baking soda and rinse thoroughly.

Casserole dishes
To remove stubborn baked-on food, put 3 tablespoons of salt into dish and fill with boiling water. Let it stand until the water cools, then wash the dish as normal.

Cleaning fruit and vegetables
Salt can help to remove the gritty dirt that you find on your fruit and vegetables. Trim them first then place in a bowl of lukewarm water, add a tablespoon of salt, swish and let the vegetables soak.

Coffee maker
Get rid of the sludge in your automatic drip coffee maker by running full-strength vinegar through a normal brew cycle. Rinse by running fresh water through the cycle two or three times.

Coffee pot
Hard water can clog a coffeepot and cause yucky build-up inside it. To remedy this, pour 225ml/1 cup vinegar in your coffeepot, fill the rest of the way with water, then run it through a cycle as usual (without coffee grounds in the filter). Rinse the coffeepot out. Fill it with fresh water and run another cycle without coffee to rinse the inside of the coffee maker.

Coffee stains
To remove coffee stains from cups or counters, rub with baking soda paste.

Cooking odours - *removal*

To stop unpleasant cooking odours from permeating throughout the entire house, boil a cup or two of vinegar in a pot on the hob. The vinegar will absorb the odours.

Other ways to pleasantly freshen the air in the kitchen are to place cloves, cinnamon sticks, allspice or another favourite scented spice in a pot of water, simmer for 1-2 hours. Alternatively, put a few slices of leftover orange or lemon rinds in a pot of water and simmer for 1-2 hours, or simply place lemon slices in an open bowl in the kitchen.

Cooking odours - *prevention*

When cooking cabbage, add a few drops of vinegar to prevent the unpleasant odours in the first place. To remove the smell of burnt food, soak a towel in vinegar, wring it out, and wave it around the room. You can also rub vinegar on your hands before and after slicing onions to lessen the smell.

Copper pans

To clean copper pans sprinkle the surface of the pans with coarse salt. Rub salt into the stains with the cut half of a fresh lemon. To clean copper bottom pans, sprinkle the bottom of the pan with salt, then take a cloth dampened with vinegar and scour away the stains.

Countertops – *grease removal*

To remove grease from countertops, clean grease with grease. Pour some oil on the grease and wipe, then put some soap on it and wipe up the remainder. Other simple ways to cut grease are to use some lemon juice, vinegar, or sprinkle with borax and scrub with a scrubbing brush.

Countertops and kitchen surfaces

To clean surfaces and countertops, sprinkle baking soda on a damp cloth. Wipe, then rinse with clean water.

Mix a small amount of baking soda with liquid Castile soap to get your countertops, sinks and tubs shiny. For a "fresh smell" try adding a few drops of rosemary, orange or lavender essential oils.

To make a fragrant kitchen rinse, add 4 drops of essential oil to 570ml/1 pint of water. Pour into a spray bottle, store away in a cool dark place. Use as a final rinse after cleaning kitchen surfaces. Use any of the following essential oils, alone or in a combination pleasing to you: eucalyptus; pine; lavender; cypress; lemon; lemongrass; lime; thyme; grapefruit; orange; wintergreen; rosemary; sage.

For greasy dirt usually encountered in the kitchen and on the walls, wash surfaces with a small amount of washing soda in water. Use rubber gloves when putting hands directly into a washing soda solution since it's very strong and can irritate the skin. For stubborn grease you can make your own scouring powder by combining 115g/1 cup of baking soda and 30g/1/4 cup of washing soda. Sprinkle and use like any scouring powder.

You can also use neat vinegar on a dishcloth to wipe grease off kitchen walls, or the hob.

Dishes - *washing*
When you don't have time to wash the dishes straight away, sprinkle them with salt to prevent any food from sticking. This will also make it easier to wash them.

To wash dishes, use liquid or powdered soap instead of detergents (which are petroleum-based), or use baking soda and liquid soap or use equal parts borax and washing soda.

To cut grease when washing greasy pans or dishes, add a few tablespoons of vinegar to your soapy dishwater.

Dishwashers
For a spot-free dishwasher rinse, add 1 cup of white vinegar to the rinse compartment of your automatic dishwasher. Wash dishes as usual. Vinegar reduces soap build-up, so repeat this cycle once a month or so, with the dishwasher empty.

Drains – *to improve drainage speed and unblock*
To keep drains running clear, each week pour 60g/1/2 cup of baking soda
down each drain and pour about 225ml/1 cup of vinegar (a bit at a time)
down after it. The combination makes lots of fizzy noises and foam. If the
drain is running slow, then repeat the process. You can stop adding vinegar
when you don't hear any "fizzing" going on in the pipes. Follow this treatment with your hottest tapwater and allow it to flow down the drain for a
couple of minutes. Regular treatment will keep your drains and pipes running free.

Drains – *unblocking*
To unclog a drain try a plunger first, and then open the clog by pouring 1
cup of baking soda down the drain followed by 1 cup of vinegar. This
mixture will help to open clogs, because when baking soda and vinegar mix
they foam and expand, cleaning your drain, and the chemical reaction can
break fatty acids down. Allow a few minutes for the mixture to do its job,
then flush with hot water for several minutes. Do not use this method after
trying a commercial drain opener because the vinegar can react with the
drain opener to create dangerous fumes.

Drains – *to freshen*
To freshen drains, sprinkle some baking soda down the drain and pour
some of your green all purpose cleaner on top. Then turn the water on
and let it rinse down. It will deodorize your drain and it will eat things that
get stuck in your drain.

Drinking glasses
Occasionally soak drinking glasses in a solution of vinegar and water to
really get them clean. It will give them a brilliant sparkle. When a quick dip
for crystal glassware is needed, prepare a solution of baking soda in
tepid-cool water (l level teaspoon to 1.2ltrs/2 pints) and brush with a soft
toothbrush. This solution is very good for glass coffee makers and thermos
jugs too.

Food containers
To remove stale smells from food containers, rinse out with hot water and
baking soda. If the smell persists, let the container soak overnight in the
baking soda and water mixture.

Garbage disposal
To eliminate garbage disposal odours and to clean and sharpen blades, grind ice and used lemon and/or orange rinds until pulverized.

Kettle
Remove the limescale coating on your kettle by filling it with water and adding 110ml/1/2 cup of vinegar. Let it stand overnight, then rinse with clean water and dry.

Kitchen bin
Baking soda will keep away rubbish odours; sprinkle the bottom of the bin, and then sprinkle again after you put a new bag in.

Kitchen floor
To remove scuff marks or grease spills from the floor, sprinkle with baking soda and then wipe with a warm, damp cloth. This is even safe for no-wax floors.

Kitchen sink
Wipe a cloth dampened with vinegar around the sink to deodorise and clean.

Kitchen taps
To clean kitchen taps, soak a cloth in vinegar then wrap it around your tap to remove mineral deposits. Allow to soak for about half an hour.

Microwave
Use vinegar to loosen food grime and clean the microwave: Place a microwave-safe bowl with 450ml/2 cups water, 110ml/1/2 cup vinegar inside the microwave and microwave on full power for 3-4 minutes (it needs to boil). Keep your microwave closed for a few minutes to allow the steam to loosen the grime, then open your microwave, carefully remove the bowl, and wipe clean.

Non-stick cookware

To remove stains from non-stick surfaces, pour a solution of 225ml/1 cup water, 2 tablespoons baking soda into a pan, simmer for 5 to 10 minutes. Do not allow mixture to boil or to boil over the side of the pan. Wash in hot water, rinse and dry. Apply a light coating of cooking oil.

Oven

Oven - *General cleaning*

To remove grease and grime and cooking spills from inside your oven, make a paste of 225ml/1 cup white distilled vinegar and 30g/ 1/4 cup of powdered laundry detergent. Heat your oven for five minutes at 350 degrees and turn off. Spread the paste around the oven, applying it more heavily to very greasy areas. Leave paste on for an hour, then use a plastic spatula to gently scrape the dirt away.

Odours - *Neutralize chemical odours*

If you choose to clean your oven with chemical cleaners, keep your freshly-cleaned oven from stinking up your house next time you cook something, by wiping it with white distilled vinegar poured directly on the sponge as a final rinse. It neutralizes the harsh alkali of oven cleaners.

Oven - *Odour removal*

Stop unpleasant cooking odours from permeating through the house whilst cooking. Boil 225ml/1 cup of white distilled vinegar with 450ml/2 cups of water in a pan on the hob. Leave boiling until the liquid is almost gone.

Oven - *Overnight cleaning*

You'll need baking soda, water, vegetable oil-based liquid soap. Sprinkle water on the oven bottom. Cover with baking soda and let it sit overnight. Wipe off and apply liquid soap with scouring pad. Rinse.

Oven - *Prevent build up of grease in oven*

Dip a sponge or cloth in full strength white distilled vinegar and wipe down all sides of the oven to prevent a greasy build up.

Kitchen

Pots and pans

Right after using the pot or pan put some soap inside while it is still hot and run water over it. This loosens up the grease and grime and most of it will go on down the drain. You may have to scrub it out a bit. Or you could put plain water in the pan and let it boil a few minutes then pour down the drain. To clean a greasy pan easily, add 1 or 2 teaspoons of baking soda to the water in which it is soaking.

To remove burned, and crusted on foods; soak or boil a solution of 2 tablespoons baking soda to 1.2ltrs/2 pints water in each pan. Let stand until particles are loosened, then wash as usual. Use a mild or moderate abrasive if necessary.

Refrigerator

Sprinkle equal amount of salt and baking soda onto a damp sponge and wipe the surfaces.

Alternatively, to clean exterior and interior walls, dissolve 2 tablespoons baking soda in 1.2ltrs/2 pints warm water and wipe all surfaces. For stubborn spots, rub with baking soda paste. Be sure to rinse with a clean, wet cloth. (This works well on other enamel-finished appliances as well.)

To clean interior fixtures, such as vegetable bins and shelves, wash in hot water and vegetable oil based soaps, rinse well and dry.

A box or small bowl of baking soda in the refrigerator, freezer, or any cupboard will keep away unpleasant odours. Alternatively two or three slices of white bread, or activated charcoal will absorb refrigerator odours.

Safety - Emergency Fire Extinguisher

If a greasy pan catches on fire, turn the heat off and try to cover the pan. Sprinkle powdered baking soda over the fire. (Fill a large coffee pot with baking soda and keep it near the hob.) An oven fire is easily extinguished by closing the door after shutting off the heat.

Stainless steel fixtures

To remove rust stains from a stainless steel sink or surface, make a paste with cream of tartar and a small amount of lemon juice. Wipe it onto the stained surface, then buff off. Stainless steel can be cleaned with undiluted white vinegar.

Stainless steel pans

Use a dry mix of equal amounts of baking soda, washing soda and borax to scrub out your stainless steel pans.

Wood cutting/chopping board

Use vinegar to disinfect and clean wood cutting boards by rubbing with a dampened cloth. If your cutting board has deep grooves, you can also soak the board in vinegar for 5-10 minutes.

Bathroom

Bathroom

Bathroom

Bathrooms no longer have to be a chore to clean. The same cleaning products used in the kitchen are suitable for the bathroom, for example, white vinegar, baking soda, and lemon juice.

Bath

Vinegar removes most dirt without scrubbing and doesn't leave a film. Use 55ml/1/4 cup (or more) vinegar to 4ltrs/1 gallon water. To remove a stronger film buildup, apply vinegar full-strength to a sponge and wipe. Next, use baking soda as you would a scouring powder. Sprinkle and rub with a damp sponge and rinse thoroughly with clean water.

Another tip for cleaning the bath is to rub the area to be cleaned with half a lemon dipped in borax, baking soda or salt. Rinse well, and dry with a soft cloth.

To help save your back whilst cleaning out the bath and shower, get a good stiff broom. This will keep you from having to bend over so much.

Bathroom deodorizer

Add a couple of drops of your favourite essential oil to the inside of the cardboard toilet tissue roll. With each turn, fragrance is released into the room. To dissipate bad smelling gases in the air, simply light a match for a few moments or burn a candle (scented or unscented). The flame from either will "eat-up" the bad smelling gases.

Bathroom floors

To clean hardwood, linoleum, tiles, and any washable surfaces use 110ml/1/2 cup of vinegar with 4ltrs/1 gallon hot water.

Bathroom glass and mirrors

To make a bathroom glass cleaner, mix 1-2 tablespoons of white vinegar with 1.2ltrs/2pints of water in a spray bottle. To remove oily fingerprints and hairspray from the mirror, dab on a little rubbing alcohol and wipe with a linen rag.

Bath/shower glass sliding doors

Use 55ml/1/4 cup white vinegar mixed with 170ml/3/4 cup of hot water to wipe away hard water stains. Help shower doors stay cleaner by wiping them with a mixture of tea tree oil and water.

Drains

To help avoid clogged drains, pour 30g/1/4 cup baking soda down weekly. Rinse thoroughly with hot water. There was a test conducted that found out that the bathroom sink drain has more bacteria than the toilet! In fact the least contaminated area in the bathroom is the toilet seat and the most contaminated area is the sink drain. Pour straight vinegar down your bathroom sinks weekly to keep them clean.

Grout

If the grout between your tiles is looking hard, dip a toothbrush in full strength vinegar and gently scrub.

To clean grout, put 345g/3 cups baking soda into a medium-sized bowl and add 225ml/1 cup warm water. Mix into a smooth paste and scrub into grout with a sponge or toothbrush. Rinse thoroughly and dispose of leftover paste when finished.

To treat mouldy tile grout on bathroom walls, fill a spray bottle with 110ml/1/2 cup hydrogen peroxide and 225ml/1 cup water. Spray onto mouldy areas, let sit for an hour, then rinse off.

Alternatively try the General Tea Tree Oil Spray described in the recipe chapter. (ie: Combine 2 teaspoons of tea tree oil in 450ml/2 cups of water in a spray bottle.) Shake to blend and spray grout to repel mould and mildew. While this formula won't take away the mould discoloration, it will kill the mould.

You may want to wear a mask and long gloves to protect yourself from the mould spores, when cleaning the grout. Dry vapour steam cleaners also work great on mould in grout.

Hairbrushes and combs

Hairbrushes and combs can be cleaned in a baking soda solution.

Hard water spots

To remove hard water spots from bathtubs, sinks and shower stalls, soak a sponge in full strength vinegar, wipe, let stand for five minutes then rinse with clean water. Alternatively apply full-strength lemon juice and let stand until the spot disappears. Rinse, and repeat if necessary.

Limescale deposit

Heat a small container of white distilled vinegar to boiling point. Then pour over your fixtures that have deposits of limescale. This will release or remove the deposit.

Metal shower heads - *removable*

Mineral deposits from hard water can cause a sputtering, clogged shower head. Place the showerhead in a pot, add enough vinegar to completely cover it. Heat the vinegar to just below boiling, then remove from heat. Allow to sit for at least 6 hours. The acid in the vinegar will eat away the deposits. Rinse the showerhead well, and it's ready to go again.

Mould and mildew

Dissolve 110ml/1/2 cup vinegar with 60g/1/2 cup borax in warm water to make a mildew remover.

Keeping your shower and bathtub dry really cuts down on mould and mildew. Use a squeegie after showering and pull the water down from the walls of the shower to keep it dry. Let some natural light into the bathroom to cut down on mould and mildew.

To prevent mould and mildew in the shower, wipe down tile or formica shower walls with a sponge or cloth dampened with water and vinegar. The vinegar will clean the walls and inhibit the growth of mould and mildew.

Plumbing fixtures

To clean stainless steel, chrome, fibreglass, ceramic, porcelain or enamel fixtures, dissolve 2 tbsp baking soda in 1.2ltrs/2 pints of water. Wipe on fixtures then rinse.

Bathroom

Hard limescale deposits around taps can be softened for easy removal by covering the deposits with vinegar-soaked paper towels. Leave the paper towels on for about one hour before cleaning. Leaves chrome clean and shiny.

If you have a removable plastic shower head, combine 570ml/1 pint white vinegar and 570ml/1 pint hot water. Completely submerge the shower head and soak for about one hour.

Porcelain
To clean porcelain surfaces, rub with cream of tartar sprinkled on a damp cloth.

Rust stains and hard water deposits
Apply full-strength vinegar or lemon juice and let stand until spot disappears, rinse. Repeat if necessary.

Soap scum and rust stains
Salt is great on soap scum and rust stains and it is a natural bleacher. Use 450ml/2 cups of water to 1 teaspoon of salt. Alternatively soak a sponge in full strength vinegar, wipe the affected area, let stand for five minutes then rinse with clean water.

Neat lemon juice can also be applied to rust stains. Let the juice stand until the spot disappears. Then rinse and repeat if necessary.

Stubborn stains
To remove stubborn stains from most surfaces, use a baking soda paste (3 parts baking soda, one part water). Apply, let stand, then scrub or wipe clean.

Tiles
Clean your ceramic tiles with a solution of 110ml/1/2 cup vinegar to 4ltrs/1 gallon warm water. Help tiles to stay cleaner by wiping them with a mixture of tea tree oil and water.

Bathroom

Toilet

To clean your toilet, use one part baking soda to four parts vinegar. Sprinkle baking soda into the bowl, then squirt with vinegar. Let it sit 15-30 minutes before scrubbing and flushing through. Cleans and deodorizes.

For removing a stubborn stain, like toilet bowl ring, mix enough borax and lemon juice into a paste to cover the ring. Flush toilet to wet the sides, then rub on paste. Let sit for 2 hours and scrub thoroughly. For less stubborn toilet bowl rings, sprinkle baking soda around the rim and scrub with a toilet brush.

Denture tablets are an excellent substitute for toilet cleaner. Drop two tablets into the bowl and clean as you would with toilet cleaner.

To sanitize and clean a toilet with a ring, spray the area down first with your homemade natural disinfectant, flush the toilet, wear gloves and scrub out the ring with a pumice stone. Use a cheap pumice (one that falls apart easily). Clean the area near the top of the bowl using a sponge with a scrubbie on one side. Then flush the mess away. Spray the area underneath and behind the seat and wipe it clean. Then wipe down the area near the floor, then the flush handle and finally wipe down and around the top and sides of the toilet.

To clean and disinfect the toilet rim, put straight 5 per cent solution of vinegar in a squirt bottle and use it to clean the rim of the toilet.

Toothbrush holder

Get the grime and caked-on toothpaste drippings out of the grooves by cleaning with a cloth moistened with white distilled vinegar.

Towel rack

Clean and disinfect by wiping with a cloth dipped in white distilled vinegar.

Water marks

To remove hard-water stains pour in 675ml/3 cups of distilled white vinegar under a running hot tap. Allow the bathtub to fill up over the stains and allow it to soak for about four hours. When the water drains out, you should be able to easily remove the stains.

Laundry

Laundry

Laundry

Do not use vinegar in your laundry if you are also using bleach as it will produce harmful vapours.

Use the washing machine only when you have a full load and wherever possible wash at a maximum of 40°C as this will use up to a third less electricity.

Wherever possible, dry clothes outside as this will also cut electricity usage.

Detergent is specially adapted to clean synthetic fabrics, and it has the added advantage of not leaving soil residues even in hard water. However, detergents are generally derived from petrochemicals, and people sensitive to these compounds may find it hard to tolerate detergents or the fragrances they are scented with.

In addition, most detergents contain phosphates, which build up in streams and lakes and upset the natural balance in waterways. This causes blooms of algae which deplete the dissolved oxygen that fish need to live. Some detergents may even contain naphthalene or phenol, both hazardous substances.

An effective alternative to using detergents is to return to soap. Soap is an effective cleaner for natural fabrics, leaving such items as nappies softer than detergent can.

For cotton and linen, use soap to soften water. A cup of vinegar added to the wash can help keep colours bright. 30-85g/1/2-3/4 cup of baking soda will leave clothes soft and fresh smelling. Silks and wools may be hand washed with mild soap or a protein shampoo, down or feathers with mild soap or baking soda.

For synthetic fabrics or blends (including most no-iron fabrics), there are biodegradable detergents on the market that do not contain phosphates, fragrances, or harsh chemicals.

For white clothes, use 30g/1/4 cup washing soda (sodium carbonate) in place of bleach. Bleach is one of the most toxic substances for the environment. Washing soda costs only a few pennies per wash load, and it is far less expensive than bleach. Along with the washing soda, add 55ml/1/4 cup of white vinegar.

For dark clothes, use 55ml/1/4 cup of white vinegar and 30g/1/4 cup of salt. Salt helps to restore faded colours, and to remove dirt and grime.

Instead of fabric softeners, which are expensive and full of synthetic fragrances, try adding 110-225ml/1/2 - 1 cup of white vinegar to the rinse cycle of your machine. This will help to rinse out the detergent completely and leave your clothes feeling soft. This is especially valuable when laundering cloth nappies as it will remove the soap residue which can cause nappy rash, and it also eliminates any lingering nappy odour.

The vinegar also balances the pH which will extend the life of your fabrics. The smell of vinegar dissipates upon drying and leaves the laundry smelling fresh.

If you wish to add fragrance to the laundry apply 2 or 3 drops of essential oil to a damp washcloth and place in the clothes dryer along with the wet laundry.

Lavender is a good choice both for its clean smell and disinfecting properties. You can also replace half of each measure of laundry detergent with baking soda to keep clothing fresh.

Bedlinen
To keep bedlinen sweet and fresh use the lavender linen water recipe on pp. 31. Alternatively, grind lavender buds or dried scented geranium leaves or dried lemon verbena leaves in a coffee mill or blender.

When changing the linens on the beds, sprinkle a small amount of this powder on the mattress (or mattress pad), then place the bottom sheet over and on the mattress.

Since lavender has bug repelling properties, sleep time is not only sweet and relaxing, but reassuring as well. After placing fresh pillowcases on the pillows, sprinkle a small amount of this herbal powder inside the cases. Another good combination is a small amount of mint added to the lavender.

Lint remover
Keep lint from clinging to your dark clothes by adding 110ml/1/2 cup vinegar to the rinse cycle.

Mildew
Dab vinegar on the soiled areas to kill the mildew. Let the item sit in the sun for a few hours and then wash separately from other items.

Moth repellent
To freshen, wash and repel moths from your clothes, add 2 teaspoons of tea tree oil to your washing machine.

Cloves, rosemary, lavender and thyme, can go a long way to keeping your stored fibres clean, fresh and moth free.

Mould
Add 1/2 teaspoon tea tree oil to your laundry for towels and other fabric prone to getting mouldy.

Nappies - *stubborn stains*
Soak or rinse your nappies in water with a dessertspoon full of bicarbonate of soda, to help budge stubborn stains. Sunlight has a bleaching effect, so simply hanging out nappies to dry in the sun will help to fade any stains that may persist on nappies after washing.

Nappy Sanitizing

Between washes, some people choose to store dirty nappies in a bucket, and soak the nappies in a sanitizing solution. Commercial nappy soak powders are available, however, for a gentler, green approach you can use either tea tree oil or lavender oil to sanitize nappies.

Tea tree oil is a powerful, natural antiseptic with fungicidal properties. To soak nappies add 5 drops of tea tree oil to a bucket of water. Lavender oil also has antiseptic properties: Use 5 drops in 2/3 of a bucket of water. Replace the solution every day for best results. Besides cleansing the nappies, the fresh smell of tea tree oil, and the fragrant scent of lavender oil will help deodorize the nappy bucket. If you do soak nappies in a sanitizing solution be aware that you do not need to wash your nappies at a very high temperature. The sanitizing solution will have already been at work killing off germs, so you could wash cooler at 40°C.

Please note that both tea tree oil and lavender oil are active essential oils and sometimes babies may be sensitive to them. Therefore, use cautiously at first, and never apply the oils directly to skin. Buckets of water are a potential drowning hazard for mobile babies and toddlers, so be vigilant about keeping them out of their reach.

Odour Removal

Reduce laundry hamper odours
If you keep a laundry hamper, add some baking soda every day to keep the hamper from smelling between loads.

For sweet-smelling closets
Mix together equal parts of dried cloves, rosemary and thyme, place in small cloth pouches or tea bags, then hang in closets or fold in with out-of-season clothing. Dried lemon peels will also do the trick.

For smoky clothes
To eliminate smells run a hot tub of water and pour in one or two cups of vinegar. Hang the smelly clothes on hangers along your shower curtain rod. This will remove smoke and other tough smells.

Stain Removal

Antiperspirant
Blot the spot with a cloth dampened with a solution of baking soda and vinegar. Wash as usual in the hottest water that's safe for the fabric.

Glue
Loosen the dried on glue by soaking a clean cloth in vinegar and saturating the spot until it's gone.

Grass
Mix 170ml//3 cup vinegar and 170ml/2/3 cup water. Apply the solution to the stain and blot. Repeat the process, as needed, then wash as usual.

Grease
To remove grease stains, either add baking soda to the wash load or pretreat the stains with a baking soda paste.

Fruit, jam(jelly), mustard or coffee stains
Rub a small amount of vinegar gently on fruit, jam, mustard or coffee type stains and wash as usual.

Tar
Wet a rag with food grade linseed oil and rub hard.

Cleaning your Iron - *Inside*

To eliminate mineral deposits and prevent corrosion on your steam iron, give it an occasional cleaning by filling the reservoir with undiluted white distilled vinegar.

Place the iron in an upright position, switch on the steam setting, and let the vinegar steam through it for 5-10 minutes. Then refill the chamber with clean water and repeat. Finally, give the water chamber a good rinsing with cold, clean water.

Cleaning your Iron - *Cleaning the soleplate*

To remove scorch marks from the soleplate of your iron, scrub it with a paste made by heating up equal parts white distilled vinegar and salt in a small pan. Use a rag dipped in clean water to wipe away the remaining residue.

Scorch marks

Eliminate slight scorch marks by rubbing the spot with a cloth dampened with white distilled vinegar, then blotting it with a clean towel.

Shiny seat marks

Brush the area lightly with a soft recycled toothbrush dipped in equal parts white distilled vinegar and water, then pat dry with a soft towel.

Wrinkle removal

Remove wrinkles out of clothes after drying by misting them with a solution of 1 part white distilled vinegar to 3 parts water. Spray the entire surface area thoroughly, hang it up and let it air-dry. You may find this approach works better for some clothes than ironing; it's certainly a lot gentler on the material.

Laundry

General Household

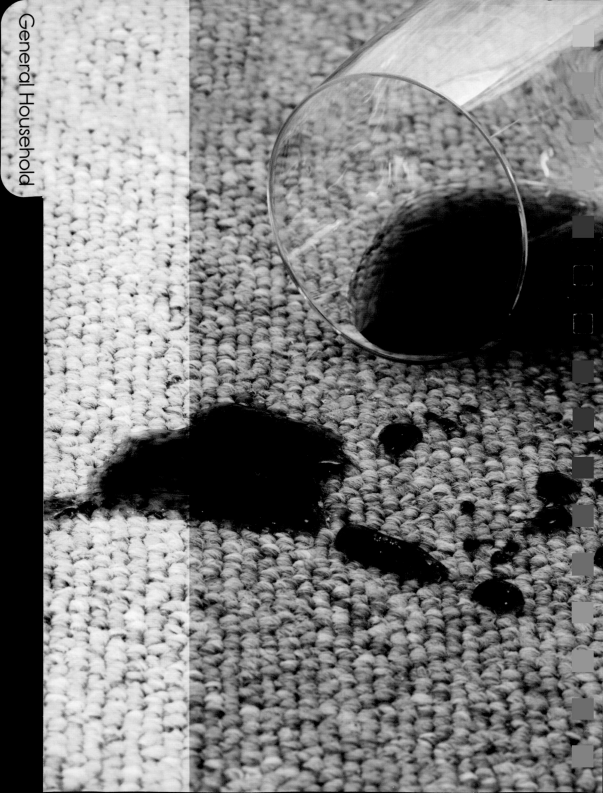

General Household

Bins
Sprinkle 60g/1/2 cup borax in the bottom of bins or nappy pails to inhibit mould and bacteria growth that can cause odours.

Carpets

Just as salt helps to restore the colour of dark laundry, it also helps to bring out the colour in carpeting, while at the same time, removing dirt. Sprinkle 30-60g/1/4 - 1/2 cup of salt (depending on the size of your rug or carpet), let it sit for 15-30 minutes, and then vacuum. You can also alternate between salt and cornstarch. The instructions are the same.

Carpets - *deodorizing*
If your carpet is holding onto pet or other odours, sprinkle the carpet with baking soda before you vacuum. If convenient, let the sprinkle stand for at least fifteen minutes before vacuuming.

For a fragrant carpet sprinkle try the following recipe: mix 175g/1 1/2 cups baking soda together with 20 drops of your favourite essential oils. You can also use about 60g/1/2 cup of cornstarch in place of some of the baking soda if you wish a different consistency of sprinkle. Place the baking soda in your mixing container and distribute the drops of oil, one at a time, here and there, throughout the powder. Don't just lay them on top of the powder in a clump. With the back of a spoon or other appropriate tool, blend the oil(s) well into the baking soda. Pour some of the powder out onto a piece of paper and use this as a funnel to pour into a sprinkle container - recycled jars with holes for sprinkling are good for this purpose.

During flea or bug season, use 60g/1/2 cup borax and 175g/1 1/2 cup baking soda, or use 115g/1 cup diatomaceous earth (not the kind used for pool filters – check the organic gardening resources in your area), plus 115g/1 cup baking soda. Diatomaceous earth (D.E.) is a superb natural product with many household and garden uses.

Carpets - *deodorizing cont/*

The fragrance choice for oils in your carpet sprinkle is personal.

Some suggestions are:

For spring and summer try 15 drops lavender oil, 5 drops rose oil, 2 or 3 drops musk oil. Lavender has a clean smell and is also somewhat of a bug repellent. Recent studies indicate that the essential oils of lemon thyme, sweet marjoram, rosemary, basil and thyme also look very promising for insect repelling properties.

When the bugs decide they prefer your home to the great outdoors, try combining 15 drops of lavender with 5 drops of citronella oil. You might wish to try equal amounts of both. In either case 2 or 3 drops of a floral musk fragrance oil are recommended to provide an overlying sweet floral scent.

During winter, the smells of pine and cedar or the Christmas smells of cinnamon and cloves invoke feelings of warm holiday cheer. Use fragrance oils to create these moods.

Carpet – *stain removal*
There are several things to be aware of before cleaning carpet stains. Firstly, when removing stains from carpeting, never apply heat to the stain because this will lock in the stain and removal will be next to impossible.

Secondly, be aware of the problem of "wicking". Wicking is when the staining agent gets deep down into the base of the carpet. When you clean the carpet, you might remove only the stain from the top carpet fibres. In time, the liquid that's left in the base of the carpet is absorbed by the fibres and works its way back to the top of the carpet causing the stain to reappear.

To avoid wicking, try cleaning the stain with your stain fighting solution of choice and then covering with a thick towel. Place books or other weights over the towel to absorb all the liquid. Leave for a few hours or over night. In the morning lift the towel and do any necessary cleaning.

Carpet – *stain removal cont/*

Finally, it is important to use a blotting action rather than a rubbing action when cleaning stains. With rubbing, you run the risk of having the stain set in deeper. You also run the risk of making the carpet fibres weaker, which can cause the affected area to wear out quicker than the rest of the carpet.

Carpet stains and baking soda
Baking soda is helpful for removing stains. Take one cup of baking soda and four cups of water and let it dissolve then put in a spray bottle and spray on stains.

Carpet stains and Club Soda
A great non-toxic carpet stain remover is soda water (club soda) . Soak spot immediately with the soda water and blot until the stain is gone. Other clear sodas such as Sprite or ginger ale are also effective.

Carpet - Coffee stains
Once you make that spill, get a wet cloth and immediately start blotting the stain so it doesn't have time to set in. Blot until you can't lift any more of the coffee out of the stain. If blotting with plain water doesn't work, there are several other steps you can take to remove the stain from your carpet.

Try pouring baking soda or salt (a coarse salt such as kosher salt works best, but table salt will do) on the stain until the entire area is covered. Leave it on the stain for at least a half-hour and then remove with a cloth or vacuum. With luck, the salt or soda will have absorbed all the liquid.

If you don't have one of these items handy, vinegar is also a worthy stain fighter. If the stain isn't too bad, dilute one part of vinegar to two parts of water, pour on the stain and blot until the stain is lifted.

If it's a big, deep stain, pour the vinegar directly from the bottle, saturating the coffee spot. Dab until the stain disappears. Once the stain is removed, blot again with a clean, damp cloth to rinse and get some of the vinegar smell out of the rug.

Carpet - Grease spots

To remove grease spots from carpets, first sop up the liquid with a sponge, then work a liberal amount of baking soda into the spot. Let it absorb overnight. Next day, remove the excess and vacuum the area.

An alternative method to remove grease spots from carpets, is to first absorb excess with a sponge, then rub a liberal amount of corn starch into the spot. Let sit overnight, then vacuum.

Carpet - Pet urine

To deal with pet urine on carpets, dab the area with towels to absorb as much as possible, wash spot with liquid dish detergent, and rinse with 110/1/2 cup vinegar diluted in 1.2ltrs/2 pints warm water.

Lay towels or paper towels over the spot and weight down to absorb excess moisture. Let stand 4 to 6 hours, then remove towels, brush up nap and allow to dry completely. Use an electric fan to speed drying. If your animal continues to stain the place, try spraying vinegar on the spot. The smell should turn him/her off.

Carpet - Red wine stains

Blot up as much of the liquid as you can, then sprinkle the area with salt. Leave for at least 15 minutes. The salt will absorb the rest of the moisture from the carpet and as a result turn pink. Clean up the salt and then clean the area with a mixture of 1 part vinegar and 2 parts water.

Red wine stains can also be removed from carpet by working baking soda in and vacuuming.

Carpet - White glue spills

Accidentally spilled white glue on rug or sofa? Remove it with white vinegar.

A good general paste for removing stains from carpets is made by combining 2 tablespoons of detergent, three tablespoons of vinegar and 1.2ltrs/2 pints of warm water. Work mixture into the stain, but don't soak. Blot with clean cloth.

Children's toys

Children's toys (not electrical or battery operated items though) can be cleaned using 30g/ 1/4 cup baking soda in 1.2ltrs/2 pints warm water. Submerge in this mixture (or wipe with a cloth dampened in it), then rinse with clear water.

China

Dissolve borax in a sink full of hot water to clean your heirloom and fine china.

Dusting

When dusting the whole house, try just a damp rag.

Fireplaces

If you throw a handful of salt onto your fire occasionally, it will help loosen the soot inside your chimney.

Floors

When cleaning floors, try a few drops of vinegar in the cleaning water to remove soap traces. For vinyl or linoleum, add a capful of baby oil to the water to preserve and polish.

Brick and stone tiles

To clean brick and stone tiles, use 225ml/1 cup white vinegar in 4lts/1 gallon water and rinse with clear water.

Heel marks

A pencil eraser removes heel marks from a floor.

No-wax vinyl or linoleum floors

To clean and shine no-wax vinyl or linoleum floors: Mix 4ltrs/1 gallon of water with 110ml/1/2 cup vinegar in a bucket, then mop or scrub your floor with the solution.

Painted wooden floors

To clean painted wooden floors, mix 1 teaspoon washing soda into 4ltrs/1 gallon hot water.

Floors - cont/...

Wood floors

Cleaning your wood floors is best done only occasionally with warm water and a drop of dish soap. Be sure your rag is only damp. Wipe or scrub, use another rag to rinse, then a dry rag to buff your surface clean.

Wood floors will avoid the streaky look when you add about 55ml/1/4 cup vinegar to your pail of water. Be sure to wring your mop out well so as not to over-wet the floor.

To clean and polish wood floors, dilute one cup of citrus oil in 4ltrs/1 gallon hot water. Use a sponge mop and mop floor. For heavy duty jobs, do not dilute.

Metal

Metal cleaners and polishes are different for each metal - just as in commercial cleaners. A universal method to get rid of rust from metals is to soak items in undiluted vinegar.

Aluminium

Clean aluminium with a solution of cream of tartar and water.

Brass

To clean brass mix equal parts salt and flour with a little vinegar, then rub. To brighten brass surfaces, rub with a cloth dampened with olive oil after cleaning. This will keep the brass from tarnishing.

Chrome

To clean chrome rub with undiluted vinegar. Polish chrome with baby oil, vinegar, or aluminium foil shiny side out.

Copper

A simple way to clean copper is to rub with lemon juice and salt, or hot vinegar and salt. Clean more tarnished copper by boiling the article in a pot of water with 1 tablespoon salt and 225/1 cup white vinegar, or try differing mixtures of salt, vinegar, baking soda, lemon juice, and cream of tartar.

Pewter

Clean pewter with a paste of salt, vinegar, and flour.

Stainless steel

To clean, rub with a paste of baking soda and water. Rub olive oil onto stainless steel surfaces to remove streaks and prints.

Gold

Clean gold with toothpaste.

Silver

Use toothpaste instead of toxic silver cleaner to clean and brighten even your best silver. Use an old soft bristled toothbrush and warm water.

Silver can be polished by boiling it in a pan lined with aluminium foil and filled with water to which a teaspoon each of baking soda and salt have been added.

To clean silver, use a paste of 3 parts baking soda to one part water. Rub the paste onto each item, then rinse with warm water and dry with a soft cloth.

When a quick dip for silverware is needed, prepare a solution of baking soda in tepid-cool water (I level teaspoon to 1.2ltrs/2 pints) and brush with a soft toothbrush.

Moisture Problems

Mould and mildew thrive in moist, warm areas. To keep these areas under control place out bowls of unscented kitty litter to absorb the moisture. Replace these once a week. To treat areas affected by mould consider using the General Tea Tree Oil Spray listed in the Recipes chapter.

To remedy mildew in books, place some cornstarch in a sprinkle container and sprinkle the cornstarch onto the pages lightly. Let it sit for a few hours and then wipe and shake clean.

Pest deterrents/control

Dust mites
Dab a few drops of tea tree oil onto a tissue, then place that in your vacuum cleaner bags for a fresh scent and to help kill dust mites as you clean.

Flies
Try this fabulous recipe for deterring flies. It smells good enough to have in any room in the home.

Fly-away potpourri
230g/2 cups lavender flowers
115g/1 cup rosemary
60g/1/2 cup spearmint
60g/1/2 cup lemon balm
30g/1/4 cup pennyroyal/mint
30g/1/4 cup pansy
30g/1/4 cup mugwort
30g/1/4 cup cedarwood chips
10 yellow tulips
3 tablespoons orris root

Moths
Use cedar chips, shredded newspapers, lavender flowers – moths don't like the smell.

Rodents
To deter rodents, wipe pantry doors and cupboards with a towel dampened with tea tree oil. You can also leave a few drops of the oil at the rodents' points of entry.

Keep things clean! Don't leave food out for mice to eat. Food, after all, is why they entered your home to begin with. Don't oblige them.

Plants

Outside air, while it can be polluted and in some cases, very unhealthy, has a great advantage in that nature will rebalance it as long as it's at all possible. Indoors, there is no "nature" to rebalance the composition of the air we breathe. Because our homes are more airtight than a few years ago, keeping our heating and cooling costs down, indoor pollution is a known health problem. Asthma sufferers, victims of MCS (multiple chemical sensitivity), small children and infants and the elderly are particularly at risk.

So we need to rebalance our indoor air with the aid of plants. Not only do plants absorb chemicals from the air, they balance the humidity and increase oxygen levels.

Compared with an air purifying machine, plants are cheaper, more pleasant to look at and they make no noise! Most houseplants will outlast an air purifying machine, too, cutting the cost even more, and they don't add to your electric bill.

Convinced? Don't just run out and buy a dozen or so plants. That can be almost as expensive as buying an air purifier! Instead, think frugally. Ask your friends for cuttings from their plants. Look in garden centres for plants which are marked down or in bad shape that you can revive. If you already have a few plants, find out how to propagate them.

For ideal conditions, you'll need approximately one plant for each 100 square feet, planted in a loose growing medium. Some soil microbes feed on "bad chemicals" (formaldehyde, benzene, tetrachloride), and working with plant roots, will eliminate them altogether.

Any houseplant will help reduce indoor air pollution, but some are more effective than others. The list of plants varies from expert to expert, but most commonly recommended are:

Ivy plants
To offset the benzene from your gas hob, keep an ivy plant in your kitchen.

Chrysanthemum flowers
These will help to absorb TCE from new paint, and benzene from new plastics and the formaldehyde from new furniture, cabinets, shelves and carpets.

Spider plants and corn plants
These absorb formaldehyde from new paper, computers, books, cardboard, and furniture.

Azaleas
Azaleas help improve the air quality of homes containing new foam furniture, foam backed carpet or foam insulation.

Spider plants, ivy, and dracaenas
These absorb fumes from oils, gasoline and carbon monoxide.

Other powerful air-filtering plants are Chinese evergreens, golden pothos, gerbera daisies, bamboo palms, dieffenbachias, and peace lilies.

Leather care

Apply cold pressed nut oil, olive oil, walnut oil, or beeswax to leather then buff with a chamois cloth to a shine. Lemon juice is good for black or tan leather shoes.

Patent leather

A dab of petroleum jelly rubbed into patent leather gives a glistening shine and prevents cracking in the winter. To shine patent leather, moisten a soft cloth with white vinegar and wipe clean. The colour of the leather may be slightly changed. Wipe dry with another clean cloth.

Shoe/trainer deodorizer

6 tablespoons cornstarch
3 tablespoons baking soda
20 drops rosemary essential oil
20 drops tea tree essential oil
5 drops lemon essential oil
5 drops clove essential oil

Mix all, then put 1-2 tablespoons in each shoe/sneaker and rub it in. Allow the powder to sit in the shoe overnight.

Shoe polish

Mix together 55ml1/4 cup olive oil with a few drops of lemon juice for a natural shoe polish. Simply dip your rag, wipe on, then buff off.

Water stains

Remove water stains on leather by rubbing with a cloth dipped in a vinegar and water solution.

Stain removal

Greasy wax stains and marks

For crayon marks, spilled candle wax, and residue left from tape and other adhesive, dab with mineral oil and wipe gently with a rag. (Mineral oil is the main ingredient of many commercial products that advertise the removal of greasy wax stains and marks.)

Ink stains

Use a non-aerosol hair spray to remove ink stains or try cinnamon or clove bud essential oil mixed with some olive oil.

Removing Labels

Vinegar can be used to remove price labels and other labels from glass, wood, and china. Paint the label with several coats of white vinegar. Give the vinegar time to soak in and after several minutes the decal or label can be rubbed off.

Vinegar also removes stick-on hooks from painted walls. Saturate a cloth or sponge with vinegar and squeeze the liquid behind the hook so that the vinegar comes in contact with the adhesive. (NB: Use these methods only on washable surfaces and washable paint).

Removing sticky residues

To get rid of sticky residues, rub a few coats of vinegar on the area and allow to soak. Then wash off with a wet washcloth and the sticky will rub right off.

Suede

Dirt marks on suede can be rubbed out with an art-gum eraser. Then buff very lightly with an emery board. Add a shine by polishing it with the inside of a banana peel, then buff.

Wallpaper cleaner

Roll up a piece of white bread and use it to "erase" marks on wallpaper.

Wood – to remove water and scorch marks

To remove water and scorch marks from wood, mix a thin paste of salt and olive oil. Wipe on the paste, then wipe off with a soft cloth, buffing slightly as you do it. Another way to remove water stains on wood furniture, is to dab white toothpaste onto stain. Allow the paste to dry and then gently buff off with a soft cloth.

Wood – scratch covers

Hide wood scratches by rubbing with the meat of a walnut. Another remedy is to rub furniture with a cloth dipped in cool tea.

Wicker

To keep white wicker from yellowing, scrub with saltwater using a stiff brush. Then let it stand in the sunlight to dry.

Windows and mirrors

Window and glass cleaning is easy with these tips: to avoid streaks, don't wash windows when the sun is shining, which can cause the cleaning solutions to dry too quickly. To avoid lint residue, try wiping with newspaper rather than paper towels or cloths (unless you are sensitive to the inks in newsprint).

Two simple cleaning solutions are undiluted vinegar in a spray bottle, or equal parts vinegar and water in a spray bottle.

Wooden Furniture

A quick and simple way to polish your wooden furniture is to use 55ml/1/4 cup vinegar plus a few drops of oil. The vinegar pulls the dirt out of the wood, and the few drops of oil lubricates the wood so that it doesn't dry out.

The best oils to use are those that have the longest shelf life. Olive oil works well. The best choice of all is liquid wax jojoba, because it never goes rancid. It is found in most health food stores. Boiled linseed oils found in hardware stores have synthetic drying chemicals in them and shouldn't be used. Use only food grade linseed oil.

Wooden Furniture - cont/...

You can substitute lemon juice for the vinegar. Organic apple cider vinegar is the best choice of vinegar, although it is not recommended for general cleaning because of the possibility of staining. If you are cleaning something that could possibly stain, use white distilled vinegar. For a homemade furniture polish cloth, dip a soft recycled cloth, such as a flannel, in the vinegar and oil mixture, and wipe furniture.

To polish wood furniture, wood floors or even wooden blinds, and to have a wonderful citrus scent, use citrus oil which can be bought from any home improvement store. For polishing wood furniture, pour a small amount of citrus oil (undiluted) onto a lint-free rag, and polish to perfection. To clean Wooden Mini-Blinds, dilute 55ml/1/4 cup of citrus oil with water in an empty spray bottle. Lay the blind out on the floor or outside on a towel. Spray the blinds lightly, and wipe gently with a sheet of fabric softener.

Outdoors/Gardening/Pets

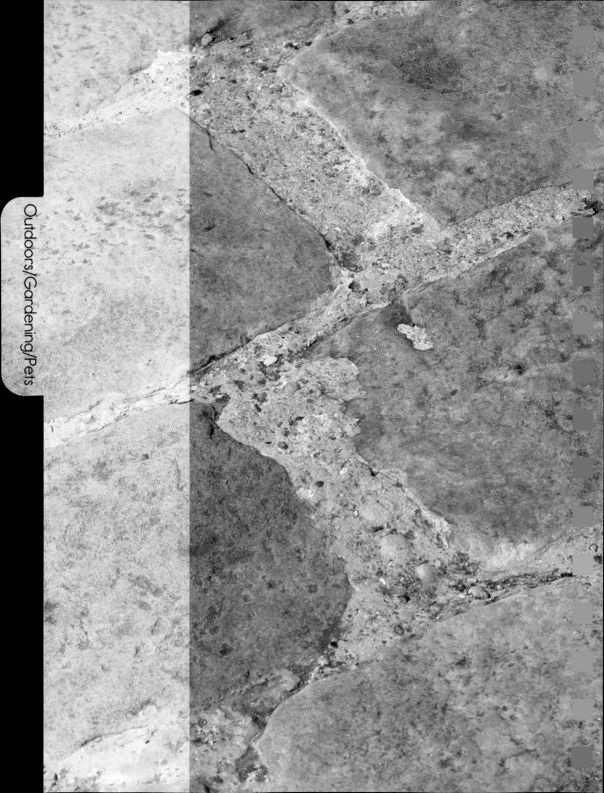

Outdoors/Gardening/Pets

Car care

Car Soap
55ml/1/4 cup vegetable oil based liquid soap, and hot water. Mix in bucket. Wash your car on the lawn instead of your driveway to reduce runoff to the street or storm sewer.

Car Wax
225ml/1 cup linseed oil, 4 tbsp. caranuba wax (available at automotive stores), 2 tbsp. beeswax, and 115ml/1/2 cup vinegar. Put ingredients in top half of a double boiler or saucepan. Heat slowly until wax has melted. Stir, and pour into a heat resistant container.

After wax has solidified, rub it on the car with a lint-free cloth. Saturate a corner of a cotton rag with vinegar and polish the wax to a deep shine.

Cleaning Chrome
Rub vinegar on chrome to clean and shine it.

Removing Stickers
To remove bumper stickers, soak a cloth in vinegar and lay it over the bumper sticker. Allow to soak a few minutes. The bumper sticker should peel right off.

Rub vinegar over the area to remove the sticky residue, if necessary.

Windscreen Frost Free Fluid
Mix 3 parts vinegar to 1 part water and coat the car windows with this solution. This vinegar and water combination will keep windscreen ice and frost-free.

Also rubbing a small cloth bag containing salt that has been moistened on your car's windscreen will keep snow and ice from collecting.

Outdoors

Bird droppings
Remove bird droppings by spraying them with full-strength apple cider vinegar. Or pour the vinegar onto a rag and wipe them off.

Bird nests
Use vinegar to deter birds building their mud nests in your facias. When you see that they are interested in building where they are not wanted, drench the area with full-strength white distilled vinegar. They will probably try several more times to make a nest. Keep spraying the area with vinegar and they become discouraged after several attempts and go elsewhere. Under no circumstances spray the birds.

Brickwork - *remove calcium*
To get rid of calcium buildup on brick or on limestone, use a spray bottle with half white distilled vineger and half water, then just let it set. The solution will do all the work.

Compost
Coffee grounds are a great source of nitrogen. Mix the coffee grounds with compost or soil to make a super slow release fertilizer.

Concrete - *drives and pathways*
Remove stains and unsightly marks by pouring full-strength white distilled vinegar over the area. Repeat as necessary until stain fades.

Decking
Mix a solution of 225ml/1 cup of ammonia, 110ml/1/2 cup of white vinegar, and 60g/1/2 cup of baking soda mixed in 4 ltrs/7 pints of water. Use a bristle brush or broom dipped in the solution and brush onto the deck to remove mildew.

De-icing pavements and driveways

Lightly sprinkling rock salt on walks and driveways will keep snow and ice from bonding to the pavement and allow for easy removal. Don't overdo it; use the salt sensibly to avoid damage to grass and ornamentals.

Drains

To "green clean" your drains without the use of harsh chemicals, pour 60g/1/2 cup of baking soda and 110ml/1/2 cup of white distilled vinegar down the drain and then cover whilst the solution fizzes. Follow this with a bucket of very hot or boiling water.

Garden Furniture - *cane and wicker*

Sponge furniture with a solution of 1 part white distilled vinegar and 1 part hot water. Place the chairs out in the hot sun to dry and this will clean and improve the appearance of sagging.

Garden Furniture - *mesh and umbrellas*

To deodorize and inhibit mildew growth on outdoor plastic mesh furniture and patio umbrellas, mix 450ml/2 cups of white vinegar and 2 tablespoons of liquid detergent in a bucket of hot water. Use a soft brush to work it into the grooves of the plastic as well as for scrubbing seat pads and umbrella fabric. Rinse with cold water; then dry in the sun.

Garden Furniture - *plastic*

Spray with full-strength white vinegar and wipe with a cloth. This will remove dirt build up and mildew and the vinegar should prevent the mildew reappearing for a while.

Garden Furniture - *wood*

Mix a solution of 225ml/1 cup of ammonia, 110ml/1/2 cup of white vinegar, and 60g/1/2 cup of baking soda mixed in 4 litres of water. Soak a sponge or rag in the solution and wipe down the furniture to remove mildew.

Insects

A number of nontoxic substances can be used to repel insects. Generally, they are highly fragrant or volatile herbs or spices. Powdered red chilli pepper, peppermint, bay leaves, cloves, citrus oil, lavender, rosemary, tobacco, peppercorns, and cedar oil can repel various types of insects.

Insects can be trapped and killed using a poison nontoxic to humans mixed with a food that insects find attractive, and spread in the infested area.

Examples are oatmeal (attractive) and plaster-of-Paris (poisonous), and cocoa powder and flour (attractive) and borax (poisonous). Old-fashioned flypaper - not a hanging strip of insecticide - is an effective trap.

To keep ants out, sprinkle powdered red chilli pepper, paprika, dried peppermint, or borax where the ants are entering.

Weed killer

If weeds or unwanted grass come up between patio bricks or blocks, carefully spread salt between the bricks and blocks, then sprinkle with water or wait for rain to wet it down. For tough weeds like dandelion, pull the leafy head off and pour a few teaspoons of salt on the exposed root and then douse with boiling water.

Pet care

Cat Litter
Baking soda in the litterbox will help prevent odours.

Cleaning fish tanks
Rub the inside of fish tanks with salt to remove hard water deposits, then rinse well before returning the fish to the tank. Use only plain, not iodized salt.

Flea Spray
Slice up two lemons and pour nearly boiling water over them, then soak overnight. Strain the liquid and pour into a spray bottle. Spritz the dog liberally and then massage the solution into their coats. Citrus oil kills and repels fleas and it makes your dog smell great too. You can also spray their bedding.

Cats hate to be sprayed, and find citrus offensive, so for felines, make a solution of 30ml/1 oz pennyroyal oil (also found at health food stores) with 500ml/18 oz of water. Sponge this solution onto your cat and massage it into the coat. You can also spray dogs with this solution, they don't mind.

WARNING: Be sure to dilute pennyroyal it can be toxic to pets if used alone. Skin that is irritated from scratching and flea bites can be soothed by applying aloe vera, nature's miracle healer.

Invigorating goldfish
Occasionally add one teaspoon of salt to 1.2ltrs/2 pints of fresh water at room temperature and put your goldfish in for about 15 minutes. Then return them to their tank. The salt swim makes them healthier.

Pet baths
Bathe pets with gentle herbal shampoos. Pesticide shampoos are overkill, since simple soap and water will kill fleas if the soap is left on for about 5-8 minutes.

Pet Shampoo

About as pure a shampoo as you can get, this recipe is detergent-free; in addition, the healing properties of aloe vera gel helps to sooth skin irritations.

450mls/3/4 pt water
2 teaspoons liquid castile soap
2 tablespoons aloe vera gel
Up to 1 teaspoon vegetable glycerin or vegetable oil

Put all ingredients in a jar and shake to blend. Wet your pet's coat, and then pour on the shampoo a few tablespoons at a time, lathering as you go. Work the shampoo in with your hands. Rinse thoroughly. Then towel them dry.

A final vinegar rinse can help the coat shine, and return the acid mantle to the skin. Combine 55ml/1/4 cup of organic apple cider vinegar with 675ml/3 cups of warm water, and rinse over the pet's coat; be sure to avoid the eyes.

Quick Pet Odour Removal

To quickly clean pets and remove "wet dog" odour, sprinkle with baking soda and brush out their fur.

Rinse for Fleas and Ticks

Wash pets with castile soap and water, dry thoroughly, apply a herbal rinse made by adding 115g/1 cup fresh or dried rosemary to 1.2ltrs/2 pints of boiling water (steep for 20 minutes, strain and cool).

Spray or sponge onto pets hair, massage into skin. Let air dry, but do not towel dry as this removes the residue of the rosemary.

Health & Beauty

Health and Beauty

Personal Hygiene and Cosmetics

We use cosmetics and hygiene products for a fairly narrow range of reasons: to keep skin moist and supple; to clean hair without stripping it of natural oils; to eliminate unpleasant body or mouth odours; to prevent skin oiliness and clogged skin pores; and simply for the pleasure of relaxing and pampering ourselves with body-care or facial-care treatments.

The following ingredients can help achieve these purposes without the use of toxic additives, synthetic fragrances, or artificial colourings.

Astringents/after shaves
Witch hazel, diluted isopropyl alcohol.

Bath soaks
For a soothing bath, add 20-25 drops of pure tea tree oil to the water. Baking soda can soften hard water and makes a relaxing bath time soak.

Deodorants
Baking soda, white clay, deodorant crystals.

Insect repellents
Several essential oils have insect repelling qualities. One great combination is citronella and patchouli oils. These can also be made into a soap with which to wash before heading outside during mosquito season.

Moisturizers and conditioners
Egg yolk, milk, yoghurt, safflower oil (for light moisturizing), olive oil (for dry skin or hair), water, oatmeal, jojoba oil.

Perfumes
Essential oils provide non-toxic fragrances that can be used to scent shampoo, and bath soaks.

Toothpastes
Baking soda, salt.

Soaps and cleansing agents
Castile soap, olive-oil based soap.

Cold, coughs and sore throats

A great remedy is natural honey, the sweetest of healers, mixed with thyme, a wonderful herb with antibacterial properties that has been used for centuries to alleviate the miseries of colds and flu. Easy to make and delicious to use:

350g/1 cup honey
60g/1/2 cup fresh thyme or 30g/1/4 cup dried thyme

In a small saucepan, combine the two ingredients and heat gently over low heat for 15 to 20 minutes, being sure not to let the honey boil or scorch. Remove from heat and allow the honey to cool. Strain out the herbs, then bottle the honey and label it. To relieve colds, coughs, and sore throats, take 1 teaspoon of this thyme-infused honey three times a day. You could also add a teaspoon of it to a cup of regular hot tea and sip slowly.

Exfoliating dry skin

After bathing and while still wet give yourself a massage with dry salt. It removes dead skin particles and aids the circulation.

Eyes

Mix 1/2 teaspoon of salt in 570ml/1 pint of water and use the solution to bathe tired eyes.

Eye puffiness

Mix one teaspoon of salt in 570ml/1 pint of hot water and apply pads soaked in the solution on the puffy areas.

Fatigue

Soak relaxed for at least ten minutes in a tub of water into which several handfuls of salt has been placed.

Feet

Soak aching feet in warm water to which a handful of salt has been added. Rinse in cool water.

Cellulite

Because juniper promotes circulation and the dissolving of fat, it can be used to effectively treat cellulite. Mix 20 to 30 drops of juniper essential oil with 110ml/4 oz of olive oil and use to massage areas of the body where cellulite is an issue.

Relaxing, Uplifting, and Purifying Incense

Burn dried juniper needles to cleanse your home of negativity and to promote feelings of relaxation, wellbeing, and positivity.

Salt Glow

Invite a friend over for a "salt glow exchange." It's nicest to do it outside where you can rinse off the salt and not worry about getting it everywhere.

For best storage, place in a cool area.

230g/2 cups fine sea salt
900ml/4 cups grapeseed, apricot or almond oil
20-30 drops essential oil of choice

1. Place salt in a widemouthed jar and cover with grapeseed, apricot, or almond oil. Scent with essential oil.

2. To use, dampen your entire body. Using either your hands or a loofah mit, vigorously but gently massage the salt and oil mixture into the skin. Begin at the feet and work upward in a circular motion. Be careful to avoid any scratched or wounded areas. When you have massaged the entire body, rinse with warm water. Finish with a dry-towel rub.

Hair care

Remove residue and styling product build up from hair: After shampooing, rinse your hair with a mixture of 1/2 vinegar, 1/2 warm water to remove all the build up and get rid of that dullness.

Health & Beauty

Insect Bites

Bee stings
If stung, immediately wet the spot and cover with salt to relieve the pain.

Mosquito bites
Soak in saltwater, then apply a mixture of lard and salt.

Poison ivy
Soaking the exposed part in hot saltwater helps reduce the irritation.

Lemon Oil
Lemon oil may be used to improve your immune system, soften scar tissue, strengthen fingernails, reduce oiliness in skin and hair, alleviate joint pain, and much more, here are a few examples. Please use only pure lemon essential oil.

For joint pain: add 2-3 drops to 30ml/1 oz of carrier oil and massage on affected area. Or add 8-10 drops to a bath.

To boost the immune system: Use 2-3 drops in a diffuser or steam inhalation as a tonic after an illness. Continue use for 2-3 days.

For corns or warts: apply full-strength directly to the affected area with a cotton swab. Be careful to avoid applying to surrounding area.

To alleviate stress: emotional distress, confusion, fatigue, PMS, and stress, use 2-3 drops in a diffuser, or 8-10 drops in a bath.

To toughen fingernails: mix 2-3 drops in 30ml/1 oz of almond oil and massage into cuticles and fingernails regularly.

For oily hair: mix 2-3 drops with unscented shampoo.

For oily skin: mix 2-3 drops of oil in 30ml/1 oz of water. Mix well, place on cotton ball, and apply to skin as a toner.

To soften scar tissue: mix 2-3 drops in 30ml/1 oz of olive oil and massage onto scar regularly.

Health & Beauty

Massage Oil

Lavender contains ingredients such as aldehydes that help to reduce inflammation, and so it helps relax tense muscles. Add a few drops to 1 teaspoon of a good carrier oil such as olive or grapeseed.

Oral Hygene

Sore throat remedy

Next time you have a sore throat, try gargling with cider vinegar!

Gargling

Stir 1/2 teaspoon salt in an 220ml/8 oz glass of warm water for use as a gargle for sore throats.

Cleaning teeth

Mix one part salt to two parts baking soda after pulverizing the salt in a blender or rolling it on a kitchen board with a tumbler before mixing. It whitens teeth, helps remove plaque and it is healthy for the gums.

Mouth Wash

Mix equal parts of salt and baking soda as a mouth wash that sweetens the breath.

Toothbrushes

These can be breeding grounds for germs. In fact, many people advocate throwing away and replacing toothbrushes every month. But that can get expensive, not to mention wasteful. Here are two simple methods for cleaning your toothbrushes, so you can get more mileage out of them and stay healthier in the process:

1. Let your toothbrush sit for 24 hours after it has dried out. This means every family member needs to have 3 toothbrushes that are rotated, since most of us brush morning and night and the brushes never really have a chance to dry out.

2. Soak your toothbrushes in straight household vinegar every two weeks. Vinegar kills most moulds, germs, and bacteria.

Health & Beauty

Cleaning

Cleaning the skin is important as it removes the dead cells from the surface of the skin. It will also remove the dust and dirt that chokes the pores on the skin. If the dust is allowed to accumulate, it can block the pores thus blocking the secretion of the glands from coming to the top of the skin providing it with the weapons it need to fight against infections, toxic agents etc. It also gives the shine or glow to the surface of the skin.

Facial scrubs

Facial scrubs help clean the surface of the skin by removing the dead skins and the dirt mechanically. The best facial scrubs contains a mild abrasive. The coarseness of these abrasives vary.   Since women spend considerably more amounts of money and time on cosmetics and skin care, we would expect that their skin will be smoother and blemish free compared to that of men. However, studies have found exactly the opposite.

These studies have found that men have fewer blemishes and smoother facial skin than women. Experts suggest that men are exfoliating their faces every day by shaving. The razor removes the top layer of dead cells daily. This allows the skin to breathe and eliminate waste much easier. This may explain why men's facial skin can be smoother than women's. Women can accomplish the same by using a mild abrasive scrub on their faces, every other day.

The right way to wash your face

1. Moisten your face with water. Work up a lather by rubbing the soap between wet palms. Using your fingertips (not the bar of soap), massage the lather into your face and throat.

2. Rinse thoroughly with a washcloth or with splashes of water. Take three times as much time for rinsing as you took for lathering. The important thing is that you remove all of the soap so any caustic it contains won't burn your face.

3. Blot dry with a soft towel; vigorous rubbing with coarse material aggravates and tugs at your skin.

For a stimulating facial, mix equal parts of salt and olive oil and gently massage the face and throat with long upward and inward strokes. Remove mixture after five minutes and wash face.

Soap and natural cleaners

Skin experts recommend avoiding soap because of its high pH. A high pH (alkaline) soap will dry the skin and diminish its life expectancy. The skin's surface is mildly acidic, having a pH of around 5. Most soaps are well over 7, and some as high as 10. Soaps with a high pH will not only dry the skin but also eliminate its acid mantle (coating on the surface).

You can make good skin cleansers from natural products. For example, products that contain vegetable oils, such as coconut oil, and water, combine with sebum and allow it to be dissolved and rinsed away. At the same time, water dissolves dirt.

Effective skin cleansers can contain a number of different vegetable oils, including coconut, sesame, or palm oils. These are safe and effective cleansers and have a relatively low pH. Stearic acid provides the skin with a pearly firmness.

Another organic product that is increasingly useful in skin care is seaweed. The high mineral content of seaweed stimulates circulation, helps eliminate toxins embedded in the skin, and leaves the skin feeling smooth. Seaweeds can also strengthen the immunity and healing functions of the skin by providing the needed minerals.

Problem skin - *acne and oily skin*

Juniper's antibacterial properties are helpful in treating acne, and its astringency helps with oily skin conditions. Combine 10 drops essential oil of juniper with 30ml/1 oz of jojoba oil and apply to face, then wash with cleanser and rinse with warm water.

Spectacles care

Use vinegar to clean your glasses: Place a drop of vinegar on the lens, then rub with a cotton cloth.

Sunburn salve

The leaves of the aloe vera plant provide a healing gel for burns that burn centres use on their patients. The gel contains aloectin B, an immune system stimulant, and penetrates all three layers of the skin. If you have an aloe vera house plant, simply snip off a two inch leaf end, slit it open, and rub the inside over the burn. Aloe vera plants, native to Africa, are very easy to grow as house plants.

Glossary of uses
Index
Conversion charts

Glossary/Index

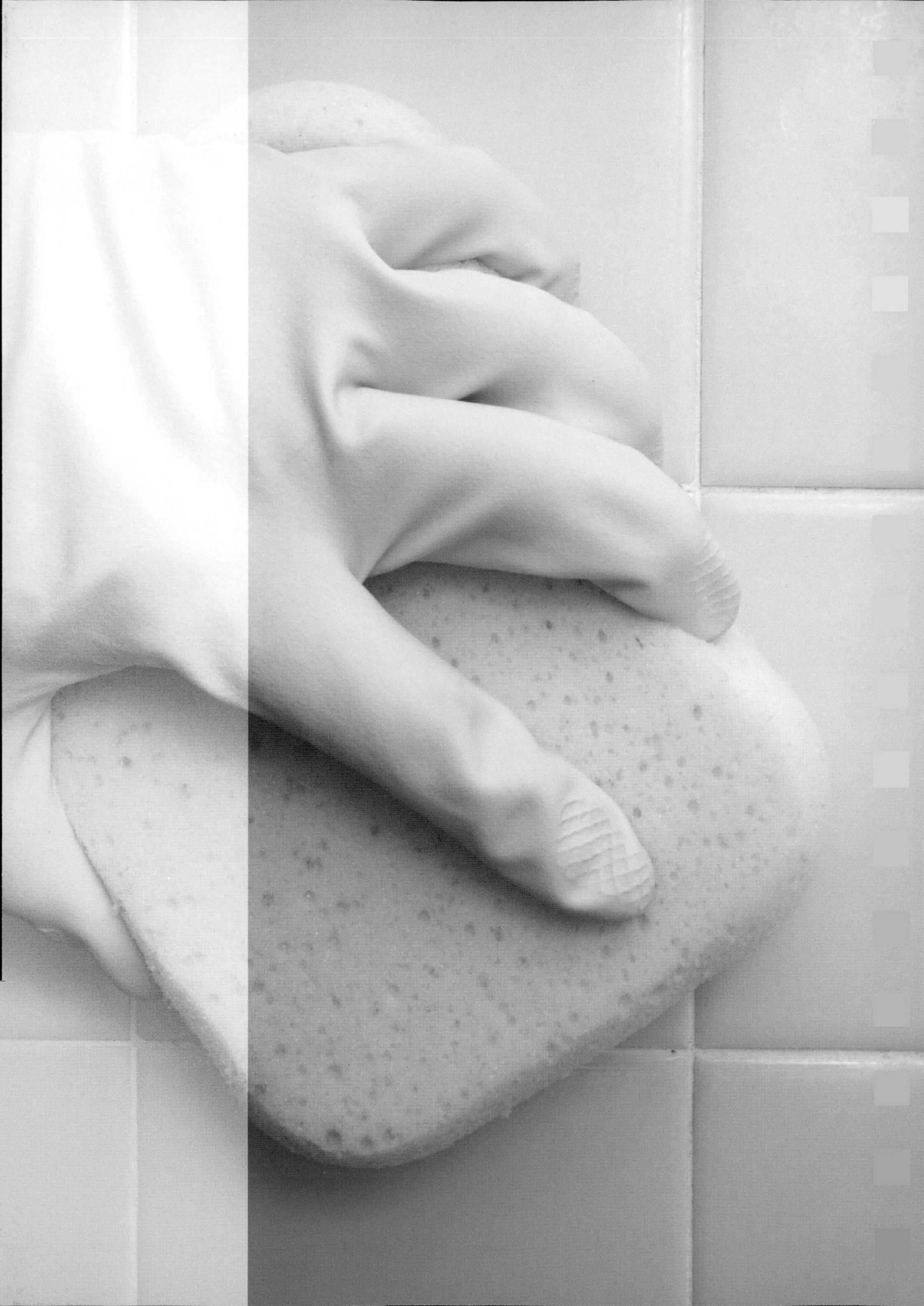

index

Index

Aa

Bb

Bb

Cc

Cc

Ff

Gg

Hh

Index

Rr

Ss

Ss

Tt

Vv

Ww

Spoons to millilitres

1/2 Teaspoon	2.5ml	1 Tablespoon	15ml
1 Teaspoon	5ml	2 Tablespoons	30ml
1-1/2 Teaspoons	7.5ml	3 Tablespoon	45ml
2 Teaspoons	10 ml	4 Tablespoons	60ml

Grams to Ounces

10g	0.25oz	225g	8oz
15g	0.38oz	250g	9oz
25g	1oz	275g	10oz
50g	2oz	300g	11oz
75g	3oz	350g	12oz
110g	4oz	375g	13oz
150g	5oz	400g	14oz
175g	6oz	425g	15oz
200g	7oz	450g	16oz

Metric to Cups

Description	Metric	Cup
Flour etc	115g	1 cup
Clear Honey etc	350g	1 cup
Liquids	225ml	1 cup

Liquid measures

Fl oz	Pints	ml
5fl oz	1/4 pint	150ml
7.5fl oz		215ml
10fl oz	1/2 pint	275ml
15fl oz		425ml
20fl oz	1 pint	570ml
35fl oz	1-3/4 pints	1 litre